EAST RIDING TREASURE HUNT

East Riding Treasure Hunt

Oddities, events, people and places

discovered by Howard Peach

Smith
Settle

First published in 1995 by

Smith Settle Ltd
Ilkley Road
Otley
West Yorkshire
LS21 3JP

ISBN 1 85825 039 0

British Library Cataloguing-in-Publication Data:
A catalogue record is available for this book
from the British Library.

Opening page: the pilgrim Rabbit, in St Mary's Church, Beverley.
Previous page: the Old Harbour and the Tidal Surge Barrier, Hull.

Designed, printed and bound by
SMITH SETTLE
Ilkley Road, Otley, West Yorkshire LS21 3JP

Contents

Bridlington and the North-East

Around Driffield

Stamford Bridge and the North Wolds

The Market Weighton Area

Goole and the South-West

The Hessle Hinterland

Beverley

Acknowledgements

Many people have assisted me in the preparation of material. For their expertise in producing documents speedily I should like to thank the staffs of Hull and Beverley Local History Libraries, and also Beverley Archives. For their kindness in providing photographs I am particularly indebted to the following:

Mr Jon Gresham (Penny Arcadia, p59) and Mrs Alison Hughes (Burnby Hall Gardens, p65), both of Pocklington; Mrs Pamela Barker (turkey weathervane, Kilham, p44); and the Humber Keel and Sloop Preservation Society (*Comrade*, p103). Mr and Mrs John Elston of Walkington have kindly given permission for a photograph and details of the architecture of their home to be included in this book.

Of the many other people who have enriched my understanding of East Riding affairs, I must mention Mr Sam Watson of Withernsea who provided me with much information on wartime coastal defences, and sparked off ideas into numberless other issues. Mr Frank Hobson alerted me to several possibilities in the Hornsea area; and Mr Arthur Lazenby of Kirk Ella was a source of inspiration generally, and in particular through his own book, *The Cobblestones of Holderness*. Mr Graham France, headteacher of Brandesburton CP School, was helpful in furnishing details on the evolution of the school. Through good fortune I learned of the French connections with Hornsea from one of the prime movers in the twinning operations, Mr Noel Bakes.

Finally I am glad to acknowledge here the help given to me by Mr Dennis Garner, the Dales Area Operations foreman, in connection with the Barmby Tidal Barrage; and by Yorkshire Water for providing technical details of water purification at Leys Hill, Hornsea.

Any errors discovered in the text are mine alone.

Introduction

Since 1978 the East Riding of Yorkshire has been my adopted county; and on retirement fourteen years later I had no wish to leave it. Much of the terrain, even on the rolling Wolds, makes for relatively easy cycling and walking, and is often of considerable beauty. It is an area of contrasts, of continuity with change. The coastline offers towering cliffs at Bempton to a shifting peninsula at Spurn whose single road is often breached by the tides. Both are rich in birdlife. The market towns have their own steady pace, homeliness and surprises. They have nurtured men and women who have left a considerable mark on the course of local history. In Beverley we have inherited a gem of an old town that is crammed with historical and architectural interest — 'a place made for walking in', in the words of the late poet laureate, Sir John Betjeman. And Hull, where I live, is still undervalued, even by some Tykes! But walk about its Old Town, see how the former docks have been transformed into a landscaped garden, a bold and imaginative shopping centre, a magnificent marina. Visit the art gallery, the theatres, museums . . . read up a little of the history and traditions of this proud city. It is an edifying saga.

Through a hundred photographs and descriptions across the Riding, this book invites its readers to explore interesting places, artefacts, memorials, etc that have stories to tell. For convenience the *Treasure Hunt* is arranged in ten self-conducted tours. Each section starts with a local sketch map identifying the recommended stopping points and preferred routes. Near each stop is a page number which is repeated in the accompanying key, with the name of the 'treasure' alongside.

It is hoped that the index will enable readers to locate similar items under such headings as People, Maritime, Artefacts, etc. Some suggestions are made, too, on further helpful reading.

Inevitably, as you make your own discoveries, you will want to stray from the recommended route. And why not? There is plenty to see. Feedback from readers would be most welcome. If you discover other unusual East Riding features — curious buildings, perhaps, or memorials, customs, reminders — please write to me via the publishers. Who knows, we may yet assemble enough material for a second volume!

Start where you will. Transport and a basic road map are assumed, and a six-figure Ordnance Survey (Landranger) reference allows each 'treasure' to be pinpointed.

Good hunting and good luck!

Overall Map of the East Riding

Bempton ● 39
Flamborough 38, 40, 41
● Langtoft 49
● Rudston 43
● Bridlington 35, 36, 37
● Sledmere 54, 55
Kilham● 44, 42
Burton Agnes 50 51
● Harpham 48
● Barmston 25
Kirby Underdale 66 ●
● Fridaythorpe 52
Lowthorpe 47
Stamford Bridge ● 57
● Bishop Wilton 64
● Driffield 46
Skipsea 26
● Millington 63
Pocklington 58, 59, 65 ●
● Kilnwick Percy 62
Lund ● 72
● Watton 53
Warley Cross ● 27
Nunburnholme 73
Kiplingcotes Station ● 60, 61
Brandesburton ● 30
● Hornsea 24, 29
East Cottingwith ● 84
Goodmanham ● 75
● Leven 31
● Mappleton 28
Seaton Ross ● 74
● Market Weighton 68
Bishop Burton 77
● Beverley 101-110
Walkington 71
● Swine 32
Rowley 70
● Hilston 33
North Cave ● 69, 76
● Riplingham
Cottingham 95
● Wressle 85
Ellerker ● 96
Brantingham 91
HULL 2-11
● Barmby 86
● Howden 83
● Welton
Brough 98, 99
Anlaby 93
● Hedon 15
Halsham ● 14
● Withernsea 13, 16
Airmyn ● 82, 88
Blacktoft ● 81
97
Hessle 90, 92
● Keyingham 18
Hollym 22
● Snaith 87
Goole 79, 80
Sunk Island 19
Easington 20, 21
Spurn 17

2. Amy Johnson's statue
3. Beverley Gate
4. King Billy's statue
5. Hull Marina
6. Trinity House
7. Wilberforce House
8. The Old Harbour
9. Old Grammar School
10. The former Maritime Museum
11. R38 Memorial
13. Withernsea Lighthouse Trust Museum
14. Constable Mausoleum, Halsham
15. Kilnsea Cross, Hedon

16. Withernsea Pier
17. The Old Lifeboat House, Spurn
18. Hourglass, Keyingham
19. Meridian obelisk, Sunk Island
20. Tithe barn, Easington
21. Pillbox, Easington Beach
22. Restored Pinfold, Hollym
24. Leys Hill
25. Trusey Hill
26. Skipsea Castle
27. Pets' crematorium, Moortown
28. Fighting erosion at Mappleton
29. La Grande Motte Garden, Hornsea
30. Brandesburton School

Kingston-upon-Hull

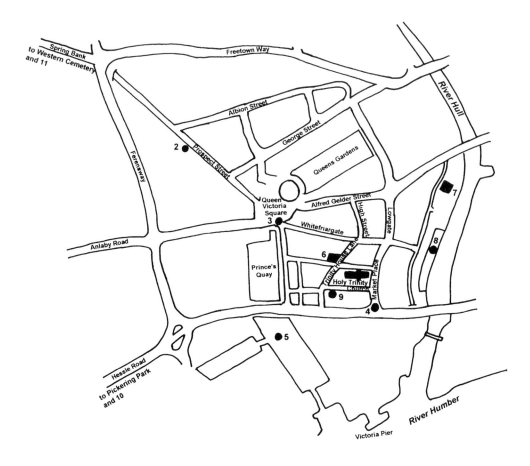

2.	Amy Johnson's statue	7.	Wilberforce House
3.	Beverley Gate	8.	The Old Harbour
4.	King Billy's statue	9.	Old Grammar School
5.	Hull Marina	10.	The former Maritime Museum
6.	Trinity House	11.	R38 Memorial

'Amy, Wonderful Amy'

The oldest of four daughters, Amy Johnson was born at 154 St Georges Road, Hull, on the 1st July 1903, as an official plaque on the front of the house commemorates. After studying languages and economics at Sheffield University she worked part-time in a London store, enabling herself to gain experience as a pilot. In 1930, flying from Croydon in her tiny single-engined Gipsy Moth, Amy became the first woman thus to reach Australia, taking nineteen days. Later she flew to India and Japan, and in 1932 made the return journey to Cape Town. After marrying James Mollison, they crossed the Atlantic together in 1933. With the outbreak of war, Amy was recruited by the Air Transport Auxiliary to ferry new aircraft from factory to base. She died mysteriously in January 1941 when her RAF Airspeed Oxford ditched in the Thames estuary.

The unveiling of this statue to her in Hull's Prospect Street in 1974 recalls the deeds of this indomitable local girl who pioneered aviation with only the most elementary support. The Amy Johnson Collection at Sewerby Hall, Bridlington, exhibits trophies, flight records and mementoes. A popular musical — our title — was based on her life.

Site: Prospect Street, Hull.

Grid Ref: TA 093291 (Kingston upon Hull, Landranger 107)

Sorry, Sire!

Excavations in 1989 by the County Archaeological Unit revealed the north chamber of the medieval Beverley Gate into Hull, together with a part of the town walls, brick-built, which once stood twenty feet (6m) high. By the seventeenth century there was a drawbridge in front of the gate, and two guard chambers to the rear.

The detail is more than usually interesting, because it was here in 1642 that the governor of Hull, Sir John Hotham, refused to admit Charles I. Although the mayor Henry Barnard wavered, Hotham stuck to his orders from Parliament, resisting all threats and blandishments to secure the city's defences and armaments. After five hours Charles retreated to Beverley; and Civil War was imminent. Ironically, Hotham was subsequently declared a traitor and beheaded by his Parliamentary masters.

On the other side of Whitefriargate, locked in between Bowlalley Lane and Silver Street, is Ye Olde White Hart Inn (c1550) where, in the first-floor Plotting Parlour, governor and council decided to bar Charles from the 'King's Town of Hull'.

Site: Hull, off Victoria Square, top of Whitefriargate.

Grid Ref: TA 096288 (Kingston upon Hull, Landranger 107)

King Billy

Sculpted by Peter Schee-maker for the sum of £893 10s, raised by public subscription, this equestrian statue of King William III in the market place was erected in 1734 and gilded in 1768. Cast as a kind of latter-day Roman emperor, he was thought to need neither spurs nor stirrups. As William of Orange he had been invited to defend the rights and liberties of the English people. He proved popular, even in Hull which had given such a hard time to Charles I during the Civil War. (See 'Sorry, Sire!' on the previous page.) Billy was an active leader, and it was in the midst of preparations for war against France that he died in 1702 as a result of a fall from his horse.

By 1734 it was clear that the Protestant succession had brought a more stable political and religious settlement, although the Jacobite movement to enthrone Bonnie Prince Charlie was smouldering in Scotland. The time was thought right to recognise what the Dutch prince had done for his adopted country.

During World War Two the statue was removed for safety to Houghton Hall, near Newbald. An annual trick favoured by some Hull citizens when fresh snow has fallen is to create lone footsteps from the statue to a local hostelry, or the public toilets close by!

Site: market place, Hull, by Holy Trinity Church.

Grid Ref: SE 100285 (Kingston upon Hull, Landranger 107)

Bobbing Masts

Since 1983, Hull Marina has become a major tourist attraction that can vie with the best in the Baltic. An older generation will recall, without nostalgia, the derelict Humber and Railway Docks, abandoned in the 1960s. But a comprehensive facelift, including dredging and rebuilding the quay walls, as well as reconditioning historic warehouses, has transformed utterly this old dock area. The marina provides for visitors a colourful and satisfying spectacle, with over 300 berths for a variety of powered craft and sailing ships. During the summer it is the venue for many events, from jazz to the sailing regattas. In the north-east corner is moored the Old Spurn Lightship, brought here in 1986 but built at Goole in 1927.

Fishermen, pictured, sculpted by Kate Noakes in 1989, stands on the quayside of the marina.

The harbourmaster's office is the original lock-keeper's cottage. Here once lived John Ellerthrope, who saved thirty-nine people from drowning in these docks and was decorated by Queen Victoria.

Site: the marina is in the Old Town, adjacent to the River Humber and Victoria Pier.

Grid Ref: TA 097283 (Kingston upon Hull, Landranger 107)

Buoys and Boys

With its attractive coat-of-arms and reclining figures of Neptune and Britannia, this splendid Georgian façade of Trinity House was built in 1753, replacing a fifteenth-century building. But, as the blue plaque at the junction of Posterngate and Trinity House Lane reminds us, the Guild and Fraternity of Masters and Pilots, Seamen of Trinity House, had started as early as 1369. By the eighteenth century, Trinity House held control of shipping and navigation, together with charitable work for distressed mariners and their families. Navigational markers and buoys are still maintained in the Humber.

From 1787 Trinity House School has trained boys for careers in the Merchant or Royal Navy, and its pupils are readily identified by their smart naval uniforms. Thoughts about its motto, *Speo Super Sidera* (Hope Beyond the Stars), should involve religion as well as geography. The chapel, opened to the public from time to time, dates from 1842.

Site: Old Town, Hull. The premises are long and narrow, extending from the Georgian front on Trinity House Lane to the entrance and assembly yard at the back on Princes Dock Street.

Grid Ref: TA 099286 (Kingston upon Hull, Landranger 107)

Hull's Freedom Fighter

No 25 High Street is perhaps the most famous address in the city; for in this large, ornate, red-brick house, built in the Dutch style for a Hull merchant in the early seventeenth century, was born William Wilberforce in 1759. At twenty-one he became an MP, and soon began to interest himself in negro slavery. Many were the vested interests and setbacks, but providentially the vital bill which abolished slavery went through Parliament just before Wilberforce's death in 1833. He was buried in Westminster Abbey.

The house, now a museum, contains many artefacts and memorabilia, including branding irons, rhinoceros-hide whips and bills of sale. The exhibition includes a display of some of the horrors of an Atlantic slave ship with negro captives chained down below deck. Hull is linked with Freetown in Sierra Leone, where thousands of families were once enslaved. A statue of Wilberforce stands outside.

Also, in Victoria Square, the city centre, a large pavement plaque outside the Ferens Gallery marks the original site (1834) of the Wilberforce Monument, transferred a century later to its present position overlooking Queens Gardens.

Site: Wilberforce House is readily located in the old High Street, Hull.

Grid Ref: TA 103287 (Kingston upon Hull, Landranger 107)

The Monks' Harbour

Between Drypool Bridge and the Humber, the River Hull widens into the Old Harbour. It was created by the monks of Meaux Abbey 700 years ago. From the parallel High Street, where medieval merchants built fine houses, it can be approached via Scale Lane, one of a number of venerable 'staithes' or landing-stages. 'Rotenhering', incidentally, can be misleading: the Rotenherings were a family of merchants! The riverside walk along a restored wooden quayside enables visitors to see moored barges, coasters and other commercial craft.

High above the confluence of the Hull and Humber looms a 200 ton steel gate, suspended like a mammoth guillotine between concrete towers. This is the Tidal Surge Barrier, built in 1980 to close off the Old Harbour when Humber tides rise dangerously.

Site: the Old Harbour is immediately north of the confluence of the Rivers Hull and Humber in the High Street area of Hull's Old Town.

Grid Ref: TA 103285 (Kingston upon Hull, Landranger 107)

A Dated Schoolroom

From 1583 until 1878, when it was vacated for other premises, here stood Hull Grammar School, replacing a medieval foundation. Doubtless the benefactor, William Gee, Lord Mayor of Hull, had his reasons for incorporating 1583 thrice, in stone, amid the 20,000 bricks which he donated — Tudor patriotism, civic pride or perhaps the simple resolve to instil at least one date into the heads of forgetful schoolboys. The carved stones include also the merchant's mark of Alderman Gee. The hieroglyphics below the date cannot, therefore, be the initials of William Wilberforce, slavery abolitionist who became a pupil here in 1766 at the age of seven! Another famous pupil was the seventeenth-century poet, Andrew Marvell.

In 1988 the Old Grammar School building was restored as a local history museum, producing lively and imaginative displays of Hull and its people.

Site: Hull, South Church Side, by Holy Trinity Church

Grid Ref: TA 100286 (Kingston upon Hull, Landranger 107)

Jawbone Arches

A row of three arches, fash-
ioned from the jawbones of
whales, protrudes through a
hedge to the left of the redundant Maritime Museum on
Hessle Road. During the first
half of the nineteenth century,
these huge bones were com-
monly sold by whaling cap-
tains for use as gateposts or
ornamental arches. Occasionally, too, whales would become
stranded on a Yorkshire beach
or in the Humber estuary. Writ-
ten records of their origins were
rarely kept, but oral tradition
links these particular survivals
with Whitby.

Another jawbone arch can
be seen at the Elms Residential
Home, College Street, Sutton-
upon-Hull. It is thought to have
been erected by Thomas Bell
(1786-1851), who once owned
the whaler *Harmony* of Hull.
Whalebone Farm, Hollym, still
has one stump.

The Town Docks Museum, in Hull's Victoria Square, has a large permanent
exhibition about the whaling history, and its artefacts include a whale skeleton, and
scrimshaw work done on baleen and walrus tusks. The building, with its three
domes, was formerly the port authority offices, and is of considerable interest.

*Site: the former Hull Maritime Museum is situated to the left of the main gates to
Pickering Park on Hessle Road (A1105).*

Grid Ref: TA 057272 (Kingston upon Hull, Landranger 107)

The R38 Tragedy

It was in the East Riding at Spaldington, near Howden, that the British airship movement was pioneered. Although it attracted some of the best engineering brains in its 1920s heyday, including Dr Barnes Wallis, it was beset by accident and failure, and finally had to be abandoned.

This memorial recalls the terrible loss of the R38, the world's largest airship, which broke in two and crashed into the Humber, just off Hull's Corporation Pier, during the afternoon of the 24th August 1921. It was returning at about fifty knots (90kmh) to Howden from a test flight over Norfolk, prior to delivery to the USA. Witnesses in the Old Town reported an attempted turn to starboard, several explosions and a mid-air split. Forty-four people died, including seventeen American personnel. The English crew were buried in this single grave. The city was in mourning for a week, but the incident has passed into the Riding's considerable folklore of mishap and death. Five men survived, including the commander, Flight-Lieutenant A H Wann.

The monument records the names of the dead: officers and the men of the RAF; the Rigid Air Detachment of the US Navy; members of staff of the National Physical Laboratory; and of the Royal Airships Works.

Site: Western Cemetery, Chanterlands Avenue, Hull. Turn left off the main path and look for the memorial at the first T-junction on the right.

Grid Ref: TA 073296 (Kingston upon Hull, Landranger 107)

Withernsea and South Holderness

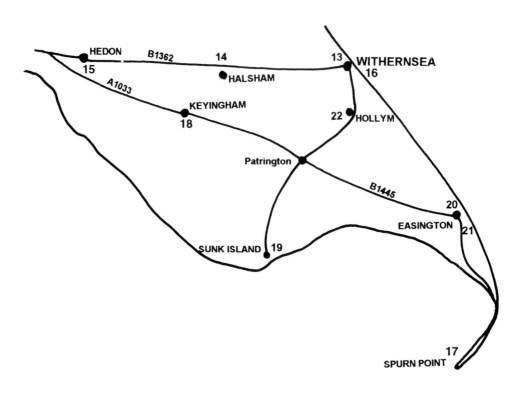

13. Withernsea Lighthouse Trust
    Museum
14. Constable Mausoleum, Halsham
15. Kilnsea Cross, Hedon
16. Withernsea Pier
17. The Old Lifeboat House, Spurn

18. Hourglass, Keyingham
19. Meridian obelisk, Sunk Island
20. Tithe barn, Easington
21. Pillbox, Easington Beach
22. Restored pinfold, Hollym

In Memory of Kay

England's tallest land lighthouse (127 feet/38.5m) was closed in 1976 after eighty-two years' service. It has since developed as the Withernsea Lighthouse Trust Museum by Dr Rolla and Kim Campbell, sister of the actress Kay Campbell who was born in the town. Their grandfather, Robert Drewery, not only helped to build the lighthouse but was the last coxswain of the offshore lifeboat.

A colourful and tasteful exhibition of Kay's life and career has been mounted, with many interesting memorabilia. There are also Royal National Lifeboat Institution exhibits and items of local history. One hundred and forty-four steps lead to the lamp room, from which, on a clear day, there are extensive views across this part of Holderness.

Site: Withernsea, at the junction of Hull Road and Arthur Street.

Grid Ref: TA 338280

A Family Mausoleum

A surprise, though a harmonious one, set on gently rising ground in the village of Halsham is this circular stone temple, built on classical lines between 1792 and 1800 by Thomas Atkinson as the last resting place for members of the Constable family, landowners in Holderness since medieval times.

Around the temple, the symmetry is simple but satisfying: seven blanked arches, plus one with a door, and with a blank rectangular 'window' set above each one. Many years ago the dome was surmounted by a cross.

Over the road is an attractive stepped gabled building, Halsham House, bearing the date 1584. It once served as the village school.

Site: Halsham, four miles (6.5km) west of Withernsea on the B1362. The mausoleum is on the northwest side, opposite the parish church.

Grid Ref: TA 271279 (Kingston upon Hull, Landranger 107)

The Kilnsea Cross

A historic monument, this much-travelled cross is said to have marked the place at Ravenser, off the shifting shores of Spurn, where Henry Bolingbroke landed in 1399 to claim the throne of England as Henry IV. Washed up at Kilnsea in 1818, it was taken to Burton Constable Hall before transferring to Hedon. The shaft has been restored. Its sculptured emblems may be of the Virgin Mary and Jesus. The top is badly eroded and its details are conjectural. Nevertheless, it is tall and impressive, enhanced by its steps and its setting on these attractive lawns.

Site: the garden of Holyrood House, at the junction of Baxtergate (A1033) and Magdalen Gate, Hedon — a small market town five miles (8km) east of Hull on the A1033 road.

Grid Ref: TA 191285 (Kingston upon Hull, Landranger 107)

End of the Pier

When Thomas Cargill designed these castellated brick towers for Withernsea in 1877, he may have been influenced by the robust gateway of Conway Castle. But there the comparison ends. His pier extended 1,196 feet (360m), concert hall included — until it was beset by storms. During the night of the 28th October 1880, two vessels were flung against the pier. The fishing smack *Jabez* sank, and the coal barque *Saffron* opened up an eighty foot (24m) gap. Repairs followed, but within seventeen months there had been another collision. Then in October 1890 another fishing smack, the *Genesta*, struck the pier, leaving but a stretch of ninety feet (27m); and in March 1893 the *Henry Parr* smashed into the rump, leaving only the towers. So Withernsea did the only thing possible: the pier-head damage was tidied — and a lighthouse was built on land!

Although Hornsea's pier, too, was damaged in the 1880 storm, Bridlington's solid stone pier has survived and remains an attraction for visitors and residents.

Site: Pier Road, Withernsea.

Grid Ref: TA 345277 (Kingston upon Hull, Landranger 107)

The Old Lifeboat House

Since the early nineteenth century, Spurn, the scene of many legendary rescues, has provided the only permanently manned lifeboat station in the United Kingdom. Nowadays the lifeboat is moored to an orange buoy just off Pilots Pier, ready for immediate action. Our photograph shows the old lifeboat house, immediately adjacent. It was built in 1923 on wooden piles at the edge of the beach, with a launch ramp on the seaward side. The short iron and concrete pier is still accessible to visitors. The last lifeboat to be housed here was the *City of Bradford III*. Between 1954 and 1977 it was launched 351 times and saved 107 lives, and at the end of this period the old house was abandoned. Like other period pieces on Spurn — the old railway, the wartime blockhouses, the two redundant lighthouses — it lends a picturesque charm to an unusually varied though often desolate landscape, shaped as few other regions are by the sea.

Site: Spurn Point, the south-west corner.

Grid Ref: TA 397108 (Grimsby & Cleethorpes, Landranger 113)

A Parson's Hourglass

Very few of these hourglasses, once common, survive, and this example at Keyingham is said to be the only one left in Yorkshire. Attached by an iron bracket to an arch above the pulpit, the glass is balanced between two wooden discs. It worked rather like an egg-timer, the sand passing slowly in a measured way from the top to the bottom part of the glass. The preacher was supposed to keep an eye on its progress and accordingly draw his sermon to a close as the sand ran out. A zealous minister might, of course, ignore it, or even turn it back again! Although an hourglass often meant literally a one hour passage of sand, this particular glass ran for only fifteen minutes, doubtless to the satisfaction of captive congregations.

The principle seems to have originated in Elizabethan times when Anglican priests, freed from pre-Reformation constraints, were sometimes carried away by their own oratory.

Site: St Nicholas Church, Church Street, Keyingham. The village is on the A1033 some six miles (9.6km) south-east of Hedon in Holderness.

Grid Ref: TA 245255 (Kingston upon Hull, Landranger 107)

Marshland Meridian

The flat hinterland of Sunk Island offers much to the geographer: land reclamation, now Crown Estate; a highly productive 'grain bowl'; and the busy commerce of the Humber Estuary. A stone obelisk set into the low wall of the river bank draws attention to the north-south Meridian line of 0^0 longitude, a basic mapping concept. Meridian derives from the Latin *meridies*, meaning midday. In 1884 the Greenwich Meridian was established by international agreement as the base line from which longitude and time zones should be calculated.

The obelisk is a triangular block set upon a square base. On the south side, a plaque shows a map of south-east Yorkshire with the Meridian cutting down to the west of Withernsea and just to the east of Patrington. Volunteers from the local school come down from time to time to clean it. The Church of St Patrick, 'Queen of Holderness' and, many would claim, the most beautiful in England, publishes a monthly magazine called *The Meridian*.

Site: the bank of the Humber, south of Patrington and Patrington Haven. Continue to follow the road to the river until the Winestead Outfall Pumping Station is reached. Turn right (west) and walk by the river wall, or on top of it, for about ³/₄ mile to reach the obelisk.

Grid Ref: TA 323183 (Grimsby & Cleethorpes, Landranger 113)

When Tenths Were Counted

Tithe barns were built by medieval landowners for the storage of tithes (tenths) of produce given to the parish priest by tenant farmers. The cause was never very popular. One tenth was regarded as too much, and farmers were disinclined to hand over the finest fruits of their labours. So tithes were given grudgingly, and even in those comparatively God-fearing times, the barn door had to be kept securely locked. In 1836 tithes were replaced by payments of rent, and were abolished exactly a century later.

The name is remembered in, for example, Tithe Barn Lane, Patrington, but few buildings have survived. This one, situated behind the church at Easington, dates from the fourteenth century. (In pre-Conquest times, Easington was 'Esa's Farm'.) Red brick, timbers and thatch have been restored, and inside, the cruck timber-framing has been secured by large pegs.

Site: Church Lane, Easington. The village is situated on the north side of the Spurn peninsula, and is gained via the B1445 from Patrington or the coast road from Withernsea.

Grid Ref: TA 398193 (Grimsby & Cleethorpes, Landranger 113)

Concrete Defences

This concrete pillbox was built about 1940 to resist possible German invaders on Easington Beach. Like many of its kind, it is unevenly octagonal, hence the nickname 'Lozenge' type. Its variety of narrow slots enabled the defenders to cover all flanks, with minimal self-exposure. Fortunately, the pillbox never saw active service, though by midsummer 1940, when an invasion looked imminent, this part of the Holderness coast was considered highly vulnerable. This particular pillbox is well preserved and overlooks the beach where concrete cubes, barbed wire and scaffold poles were deployed as anti-tank measures.

Other World War Two defences are readily found at Withernsea, where a pillbox has been incorporated into the promenade wall; at Hilston, Mappleton and particularly at Spurn, where gun and searchlight emplacements can still be identified.

Site: Easington Beach, about a quarter of a mile to the south of the approach road. Easington village, reached via the B1445 from Patrington or the coast road from Withernsea, lies at the northern end of the Spurn peninsula.

Grid ref: TA 408187 (Grimsby & Cleethorpes, Landranger 113)

A Cobbled Pinfold

Skilfully restored in 1982, this circular wall is about thirty yards round and encloses a small rest garden, mainly for the use of older residents. It is a reminder of pre-First World War days when farm animals, especially cattle and sheep, strayed from fields and roadside tetherings, to be impounded by a local keeper until the owner paid a fine for their return. The pinfold gains interest by being built from local cobbles, except at the entrance where the edges are rendered vertical by the use of stone.

But because stone, and even timber, have been hard to find in Holderness, cobbles have for centuries been used for building. Generally ovoid in shape, and of varied colours, cobbles originated in glacial boulder clays; and until prohibition in 1910 were readily available from the beach. Many churches in this coastal strip have some cobbled walls. So have many farm buildings, houses and garden walls. Two miles (3.2km) north of Hornsea, the medieval market cross at Atwick has a substantial cobbled base.

Another pinfold, restored in 1973, is located at Windmill Hill, Driffield.

Site: Northside Road, Hollym, off the A1033 from Withernsea.

Grid Ref: TA 345253 (Kingston upon Hull, Landranger 107)

Hornsea and North Holderness

24. Leys Hill
25. Trusey Hill
26. Skipsea Castle
27. Pets' crematorium, Moortown
28. Fighting erosion at Mappleton
29. La Grande Motte Garden, Hornsea
30. Brandesburton School
31. White Cross, Leven
32. Swine Post Office
33. Storr's Tower, Hilston

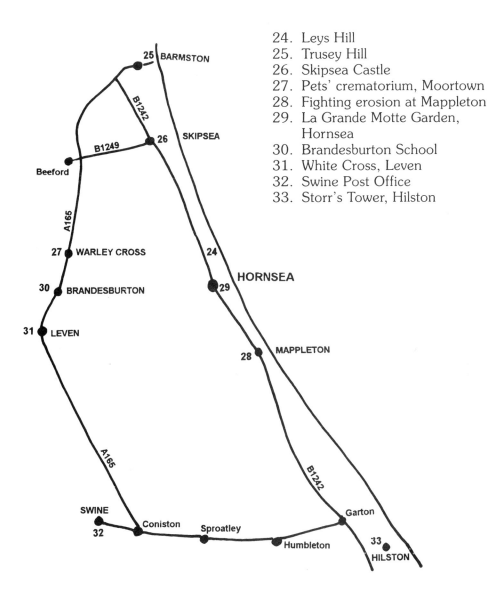

A Fire and Water Monument

Victorian engineers built this waterworks at Leys Hill in 1878 to serve the developing town of Hornsea. Prior to storage, water extracted from wells some 260 feet (79m) below the surface chalk was allowed to cascade over 'purifying steps' (on the lower left) as part of the aeration process to oxidise traces of iron. The chimney provided an outlet for gases from the pump engines. The tall, rounded windows and variegated brickwork added an aesthetic appeal; and the open hillside position near the sea makes the building a dominant landmark.

By the end of the century, 56,000 gallons (257,600 litres) of water — a day's supply — could be stored in these towers, 100 feet (30m) above the town. But Leys Hill, like subsequent boreholes, was criticised over the hardness and salinity of its water, and of its purification arrangements. In 1927 they were all closed down and Hornsea's water was then bought from Hull Corporation. Eventually the pumps and pipes were removed from Leys Hill, and the building was remodelled as an incinerator for the town's rubbish. Finally, a new waste disposal plant was built alongside. So the original building remains, a solid and indeed a noble monument to changing times and technologies.

Site: Atwick Road (B1242), Leys Hill, Hornsea.

Grid Ref: TA 196486 (Kingston upon Hull, Landranger 107)

Death Top

Not without reason has Trusey Hill at Barmston gained this label. Rising to the south of the village, its crowning circle of dead elm trunks was put there by a previous landowner in memory of trees killed by Dutch elm disease. Much has happened on this site, for here was an ancient monastery and a possible Viking burial. Some older folk maintain that a First World War gun carriage, washed upon on the beach, was buried here; and the occasional skeleton has been found. It is hard to know what to believe. Was Trusey itself natural or man-made? We can be sure, at least, about the trees, alternatively known in this locality as 'Woodhenge'.

Site: Barmston is about six miles south of Bridlington, off the A165. A good vantage point for the approach to Trusey Hill is the village hall and neighbouring field, on the south-western side of the village.

Grid Ref: TA 163587 (Kingston upon Hull, Landranger 107)

A Feudal Haunt

Skipsea Brough presents a fine example of an early Norman motte and bailey castle. The raised earth motte, or mound, was built to accommodate a strongly fortified keep, surrounded by a bailey courtyard and outer ditches and defences. Skipsea's earthworks are still prominent, the mound raised some thirty-five feet (10.5m), and the south-western ramparts remain formidable. The original nine acre (3.5ha) site was huge. The castle was built by a Flemish adventurer, created Lord of Holderness after the Conquest, one Drogo de Bevere, whose baronial integrity was soon in doubt. He allegedly poisoned his wife, the king's niece, who has been rumoured to be the White Lady haunting the castle. He then fled to France with funds given by the king for domestic purposes.

In later years there were more troubles. After a rebellion in 1221, Henry III ordered the Albemarles, the new lords, to destroy the castle. They did so, re-establishing themselves in another stronghold at Burstwick, three miles (4.5km) east of Hedon.

Another site worth inspection is the Percy castle close to Leconfield (two miles/ 3km north of Beverley), where a rectangular moat remains. At Aughton, just north of Bubwith in the Derwent valley, is a motte associated with Robert Aske and the Pilgrimage of Grace in 1536.

Site: Skipsea Brough is a quarter of a mile (0.4km) west of the village of Skipsea, off the B1249.

Grid Ref: TA 162551 (Kingston upon Hull, Landranger 107)

A Wayside Crematorium

In many villages, redundant chapels have been put to new uses. At Fangfoss the Wesleyan (1837) and Primitive Methodist (1865) have become workshops; similarly at Market Weighton with the oldest Wesleyan chapel in Yorkshire (1786). At Brough the Wesleyan chapel (1852) is now the station cafe. In very many cases a commodious chapel has become a private house.

But this former Primitive Methodist building (1870) at Moortown, standing isolated from any community, has for many years operated as a pets' crematorium. In an adjacent border are trees and memorials to departed animals.

This chapel was once well known to a Hornsea lady, Rose Carr (1843-1913), who earned a living as a carrier but was also a renowned chapel preacher, and an extremely powerful woman who had put strong men to flight. Rose was devoted to all animals, and had a way with difficult ones. She would have regretted the loss of the chapel for public worship, but — who knows? — she might well have assisted at these sad last rites.

Site: the Primitive Methodist chapel, Moortown, Brandesburton parish, a quarter of a mile (0.4km) south of Warley Cross on the A165.

Grid Ref: TA 125505 (Kingston upon Hull, Landranger 107)

Landscaping Against Erosion

Since Roman times, more than thirty settlements near the soft clay cliffs of Holderness have been washed away by these remorseless tides. A notice on the corner house at Kilnsea crossroads comments thus:

'Built 1847   534 yards from the sea
Restored 1994   190 yards from the sea'

Further up the coast, Mappleton's plight has resulted in a Coast Protection Works funded by various bodies like the county council and the EC. Huge earth embankments now bolster the crumbling cliffs, and an inverted T-shaped groyne of granite boulders has been constructed to withstand the tides. This bold attempt at coastal landscaping is at once practical and attractive, so that the village has become a minor tourist venue, complete with an extensive car park and vantage points.

Site: Mappleton, two miles south of Hornsea on the B1242.

Grid Ref: TA 227439 (Kingston upon Hull, Landranger 107)

Twinned Gardens

Why should paths in the shape of the Cross of Lorraine, with a four-sided cobbled pyramid at its centre, feature in this unusual circular garden on the front at Hornsea? During the Second World War an armoured division of the Free French Army was billeted in Hornsea, while training for their country's forthcoming liberation. Decades passed . . . and eventually representations were received from a number of old soldiers living in the new town of La Grande Motte, near Montpellier. Twinning arrangements were established and signed in May 1981. This La Grande Motte Garden was presented to the people of Hornsea by the French town six years later. The pyramid is a symbol of the architec-

tural shape of many public buildings and private flats in La Grande Motte.

Some 180 yards (200m) south is Beacon Garden, of similar size but with a central beacon holding a shield. On one side is displayed the escutcheon of Holderness Borough Council: a mural crown, topped with a sailing ship, above a central shield with sun, sea and two Yorkshire roses, all flanked by a supporting mermaid and triton. On the other side are Hornsea's distinctive bearings — the sun rising over the sea, the Mere and the town.

Site: the South Promenade, Hornsea, on the green between the police station and the seafront.

Grid Ref: TA 210476 (Kingston upon Hull, Landranger 107)

A Capital Foundation

Few schools outside the metropolis can claim to owe their foundation to the City of London. In 1601 Anna, Lady Dacre had left Brandesburton Manor in trust for her foundation, Emmanuel Hospital, Westminster. But in 1841 the hospital site had to be sold for improvements to be made in the neighbourhood of Buckingham Palace. As trustees of the Dacre Charity, the lord mayor and aldermen decided that part of the money raised should be used to build a parochial school on the original Brandesburton estate. At a time when state grants for elementary education were only just beginning, it is remarkable that the Brandesburton school should be built over two centuries after its sponsor's death — and via London!

A further interesting coincidence: just beyond the gate to St Mary's churchyard nearby lies Dr John Hymers, sometime rector, who died in 1887, leaving a considerable fortune for the endowment of Hymers College in Hull.

Site: Main Street, Brandesburton, opposite an ancient and picturesque cross. The village lies on the A165, seven miles (11km) west of Hornsea.

Grid Ref: TA 119477 (Kingston upon Hull, Landranger 107)

White Cross

Standing behind an ancient cross, this isolated building, castellated and with pointed arches on its doors and windows, remains an impressive Gothic landmark — as its founders doubtless intended. It was erected about 1761 as a toll house to mark the east end of the new turnpike road to operate between Leven and Norwood, Beverley. Local trustees led by Hugh Bethell from nearby Rise were entrusted with the maintenance of the five and a half mile (9km) stretch of road, and for the establishment of intermediate toll-bars near Hull Bridge and at Meaux Lane End, Routh. North of White Cross and Leven, the old coach road went on to Bridlington, but an extended turnpike, though planned, never operated.

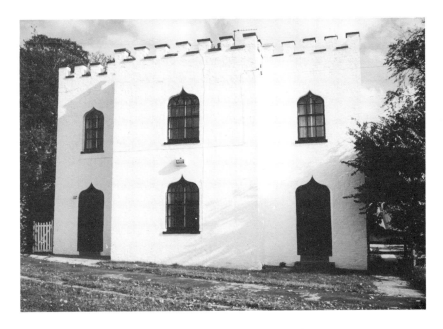

The progressive reduction of tolls, in the hope of encouraging more paying travellers, brought financial difficulties, exacerbated by competition from the Hull to Hornsea railway after 1864, and in 1867 the trust was wound up. From 1888, road repair was taken over by the new county councils.

White House has witnessed many local changes and diversions. In 1993 the new Leven bypass detached it from a busy roundabout.

Site: the junction of the A1035 from Beverley and the A165 Bridlington-Skirlaugh road about half a mile (0.8km) south of Leven.

Grid Ref: TA 109438 (Kingston upon Hull, Landranger 107)

Swine and Sheep

We may never finally know whether the village of Swine's name derived from Swain, a Saxon warrior; or Zwine, near Stettin (Germany) in Saxon times; or simply from pigs.

There is considerable enthusiasm in Swine for pigs. At the annual street gala in August, the pig stall gets bigger every year! In this part of Holderness, there are probably more pigs than people. And it is widely known, though not universally appreciated, that pig slurry is sprayed onto the fields.

Understandable, therefore, is this pig's crest in black and white outside the post

office. And there are more animal signs. A few yards down the road, the entrance to the old forge was horseshoe-shaped. In St Mary's Church, behind a pulpit dated 1619, are eight misericord seats, one showing a griffin biting its tail. On another a nun's head is between two creatures with long claws.

A Cistercian priory for nuns once stood nearby. And to the north-west, almost within discreet waving distance, stood Meaux Abbey — a Cistercian foundation once as big as Fountains, but now gone — famous for sheep rearing and in medieval times sending prodigious numbers of fleeces to Flanders.

Site: Swine is 1¾ miles (3km) west of Coniston off the A165 Hull-Skirlaugh road.

Grid Ref: TA 136358 (Kingston upon Hull, Landranger 107)

An Admiral's Look-Out

John Storr, son of a Hedon magistrate, joined the navy, saw service in many parts of the world, and became an admiral. In his retirement he returned to Holderness; and about 1750 had this brick tower built on a mound near the coast at Hilston, so that he could watch the ships come and go. The tower, standing a little isolated in a field a few hundred yards north-west of the village, is about fifty feet (15m) high and has seven sides with a rounded wall facing north. Several windows have been bricked up. On the south side, a door is firmly bolted. Above it a stone inset, leafily edged, is somewhat eroded but depicts two birds.

As well as serving a distinguished sailor, the tower is an obvious landmark, and was once a navigational aid to offshore vessels. Half a mile (0.8km) away, the church was built as recently as 1956, replacing an earlier one that somehow suffered bomb damage during the Second World War.

Site: Hilston, in a field to the north-west of the village.

Grid Ref: TA 286338 (Kingston upon Hull, Landranger 107)

Bridlington and the North-East

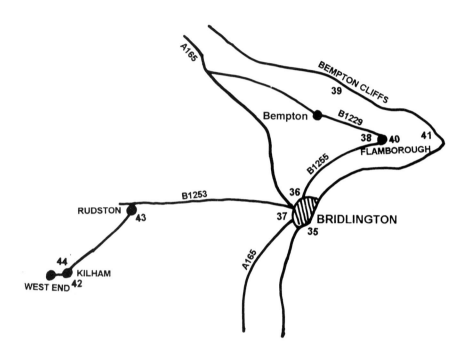

35. Lawrence of Arabia sundial, Bridlington
36. The Bayle, Bridlington
37. Market Place, Bridlington Old Town
38. Book of service, Flamborough
39. Bempton Cliffs
40. Constable Tower, Flamborough
41. Toposcope, Flamborough cliffs
42. Wayside pump, Kilham
43. The Rudston monolith
44. Turkey weathervane, Kilham

The Lawrence of Arabia Link

A simple sundial overlooking Bridlington Harbour commemorates the fact that Aircraftman T E Shaw, alias Lawrence of Arabia, scholar and hero extraordinary, was based here a few months before his death. After spending some years actively supporting the Arab struggle against Turkish domination in the Middle East, and incidentally achieving the rank of colonel in the British Army, Lawrence deliberately chose to join and remain in the ranks of the RAF in order to obtain a kind of anonymity. He had two spells in Bridlington — six weeks during the summer of 1932, and three months immediately prior to leaving the service in February 1935.

The marine craft workshops where he was employed as mechanic/designer were at Gummers Landing, by the South Pier. He lodged just across the road in the tower room of the Ozone Hotel, now the Royal Yorkshire Yacht Club.

Lawrence and his motorcycle were frequently to be seen roaring through the towns and villages of the East Riding. He particularly enjoyed his visits to his friend Flight Lieutenant Simms at White Cottage, Eastgate, Hornsea. Tragically, Lawrence died after a motorcycle accident in Dorset in May 1935 — a many-sided genius, brave, modest, elusive.

Site: the South Cliff Gardens, Bridlington, overlooking the harbour.

Grid Ref: TA 183664 (Scarborough & Bridlington, Landranger 101)

The Bayle

Built in 1388 as a fortified gatehouse to the Augustinian priory church of St Mary in Bridlington, the Bayle survived Henry VIII's dissolution. Its roomy archway has a vaulted roof, above which is the oak-beamed court room, still used for meetings of the historically important Lords Feoffees, who still administer manorial property.

The Bayle has been used for many other purposes — a prison, a chapel, a soldiers' billet, a school and latterly a museum teeming with local artefacts. There are rooms devoted to agriculture, military memorabilia, Victoriana, kitchen utensils and a cobbler's shop.

The black and white halves of the town's coat-of-arms, shown above the gateway, are thought to derive from the Augustinian connection, with the three Bs symbolising the Trinity.

Site: Bridlington Old Town, adjacent to the priory church.

Grid Ref: TA 182682 (Scarborough & Bridlington, Landranger 101)

A Punishing Place

Several interesting bygone instruments of punishment are to be found in the market place of this old quarter of Bridlington. Outside the Packhorse Inn, a set of stocks and a pillory have been rebuilt to show where and how wrongdoers (petty thieves, dishonest traders and unvirtuous women) were once shackled and pelted with rubbish or worse. Just round the corner of the ancient High Street, inside the priory church a 'joug' (from Latin *jugum* or joke) is displayed under the south-west tower. Up to 300 years ago this iron collar was used to chain scolds — wives who talked too much — outside the church gates, where they would be seen by every passer-by. Curiously, perhaps, the last prior, William Wood, was himself hanged for treason in 1537 for taking part in the Pilgrimage of Grace against Henry VIII's suppression of the monasteries.

Site: the market place, Old Town, Bridlington.

Grid Ref: TA 180682 (Scarborough & Bridlington, Landranger 101)

The Book of Service

This turntable stand with thirteen hanging boards in the Church of St Oswald, Flamborough, details every local organisation that contributed to the war effort from 1939 to 1945. Apart from the direct war service of soldiers, sailors and airmen, tribute is paid to the Merchant Navy, the Home Guard, the WRNS, the Royal Observer Corps, RNLI, special constables, air raid wardens, National Fire Service, St John Ambulance Association, fire guards, knitting leagues, the WVS, land girls, munition workers, British Red Cross, coastguards, organisers of social events, canteen workers, fundraisers and even children who collected paper, metals and old bones.

Designed in 1946 by A E Cracroft, it is a remarkably comprehensive and inspired

collection, reminding posterity of one village's collective efforts to win.

Site: St Oswald's Church, Flamborough.

Grid Ref: TA 227703 (Scarborough & Bridlington, Landranger 101)

Climmers' Cliffs

This area of chalk cliffs at Bempton, four hundred feet (120m) high, is Heritage Coast and a reserve of the Royal Society for the Protection of Birds. During the summer an immense cliffside clamour is sent up by kittiwakes, guillemots, razorbills, fulmar, puffin and, of course, gulls by the thousand. Bempton is the only gannet colony on the British mainland, and the sight of one of these birds, with its six foot (2m) wingspan, diving for fish is spectacular.

Until Parliament stopped the enterprise in 1954, local men ('climmers') were lowered by winches and ropes down these daunting cliffsides to scoop eggs off the ledges and store them in linen bags attached to waist or shoulder. Most of the birds' eggs were sold for food, or bought by West Riding industrialists for use in the chemical treatment of animal hides.

Site: Bempton cliffs are three miles (5km) north of Bridlington (B1255 to Flamborough, then B1229).

Grid Ref: TA 200740 (Scarborough & Bridlington, Landranger 101)

The Danish Connection

In a field behind Flamborough's war memorial stands this somewhat forlorn chalk tower, still about twenty feet (6m) high, once the castle of the Constable family. Legend says that many centuries ago the head of the family would march to the cliff edge once a year, and fire out to sea, in the general direction of Denmark, an arrow tipped with a gold coin as a token rent to their former overlords. A regular performer at this ceremony was Sir Marmaduke Constable, who lived through six reigns and fought at the Battle of Flodden in 1513 at the age of seventy.

So many ancient links, including forms of speech, have persisted that during the nineteenth century Flamborough became known as Little Denmark. In 1846 scholars were sent by the Danish king to research interesting verbal similarities. 'Flane', for a start, meant arrow in Norse!

Site: Tower Street, Flamborough

Grid Ref: TA 226706 (Scarborough & Bridlington, Landranger 101)

That Moonlit Sea Battle

Situated only a few yards from the cliff edge at Flamborough, this toposcope, erected in 1959, commemorates the night battle fought on the 23rd September 1779 during the American War of Independence. Off this treacherous coast the American privateer John Paul Jones intercepted two British frigates, the *Serapis* and the *Countess of Scarborough*, confident that he could outfire them and so prey on the Baltic convoy they were escorting. The five hour shelling was watched by local people from vantage points on the cliffs. Jones won a pyrrhic victory, for his ship, *Le Bonhomme Richard*, sank the next day. Although the *Serapis* blew up when gunpowder ignited, Captain Richard Pearson RN was knighted by King George III for gallantly frustrating the American's grand design.

The toposcope reminds us that John Paul Jones became known as the Father of the American Navy — and that from this fixed point, both John o' Groats and Lands End are 362 miles (580km) distant.

Site: Flamborough cliffs, near the new lighthouse, are approached via Lighthouse Road from the village.

Grid Ref: TA 254706 (Scarborough & Bridlington, Landranger 101)

A Wayside Pump

Only an older generation will recall the days before piped water, although many village pumps have been conserved. Some were in use until after the Second World War, as were wells and even ponds; and local folk, armed with pails, pots and pancheons would often queue twice a day to draw water. A notice by the Star and Garter Inn at North Dalton (seven miles/11km south-west of Driffield) records the position thus:

'Since time out of mind the people of North Dalton used this spring fed pond to collect water. Wagons, carts and stock entered down a slope in this corner'.

At West End, a scattered settlement to the west of Kilham, this very rural pump

was in regular use until 1947. It stands about eight feet (2.4m) high, and its black, cast iron frame remains in good condition. The main users were local farmers, tenants and a number of cottage dwellers. But during the nineteenth century at steam threshing times, much extra water was needed. As with the pump opposite Kilham Church, this one had a stand for the operator to mount in order to work the handle.

Another intriguing pump in this area is Black Jack at Burton Fleming crossroads which, exceptionally, has two handles and a dark wooden casing.

Site: West End is on a minor road immediately to the west of Kilham. These communities are situated some two miles (3km) north of the A166 road between Driffield and Bridlington.

Grid Ref: TA 046648 (Scarborough and Bridlington, Landranger 101)

England's Tallest Monolith

Rudston takes its name from this colossal 'rood-stone' which is situated near the east end of All Saints Church. It stands twenty-five feet (7.5m) above ground and is believed to be embedded to a similar depth. If so it would weight over forty tons. At ground level its circumference is sixteen feet (5m). The top, capped against the weather, may once have supported a cross. Geologically, it is a gritstone, an erratic that could, somehow, have been dragged from Cayton Bay ten miles (16km) to the north, or even deposited by a glacier during the last ice age.

An old tale, careless of which came first, says that the Devil threw the stone at the church and just missed! Doubtless there was once a religious significance — a tombstone to a local chieftain, perhaps, or a focus of tribal worship. Certainly for many centuries this has been a sacred site.

A noteworthy grave on the western side is that of Winifred Holtby (1898-1935), born at Rudston House and author of *South Riding*.

Other interesting stones in East Riding churchyards are the wart stone at Barmby Moor, on the A1079, two miles (3km) west of Pocklington. Rainwater collected from its crevices is said to cure warts! A large and curiously shaped boulder may be seen at the rear of Sproatley Church (on the B1238 road, midway between east Hull and Aldbrough, near the coast).

Site: All Saints Church, Rudston is near the B1253 in the north-east corner of the village, five miles (8km) west of Bridlington.

Grid Ref: TA 097677 (Scarborough & Bridlington, Landranger 101)

Church Turkeys

Turkey lore and turkey breeding are well established in the East Riding. Legend credits William Strickland with bringing some of the birds back to his native Boynton (three miles/5km west of Bridlington) after his voyage to North America with Cabot. The proud turkey cock forms the basis of the family crest, which can be seen adorning the lectern in St Andrew's Church at Boynton. In Flamborough Church the turkey is also part of the Constable crest.

But gloriously at the top of Kilham Church we find the turkey motif on the weathervane, white on one side, black on the other; here it is pictured being fixed by Mr Keith Dodsworth. As the plaque in the porch explains: 'The present weathervane in the form of a turkey was provided thanks to the generosity of Raymond W Twiddle, born in this parish and now resident at Knapton Hall'. It was dedicated by the vicar on 2nd October, 1990.

Site: Kilham is situated some seven miles north-east of Driffield. It can be reached from the B1248 to the west; from the A166 to the south; or, from Bridlington, the B1253 which runs also through Boynton.

Grid Ref: TA 065644 (Scarborough & Bridlington, Landranger 101)

Around Driffield

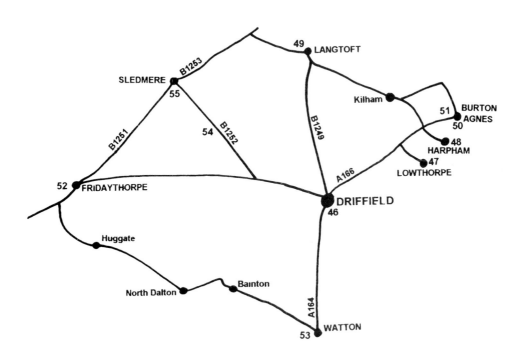

46. Riverhead, Driffield
47. Family tree tomb, Lowthorpe
48. Two famous wells, Harpham
49. The Langtoft floods
50. Norman manor house, Burton Agnes

51. Gatehouse, Burton Agnes Hall
52. Bells with Latin inscriptions, Fridaythorpe
53. Watton Priory
54. The Sykes Monument
55. The Waggoners' Memorial

Riverhead, Driffield

With the establishment of the Driffield Navigational Canal in 1770, the town became a minor inland port, linked via Wansford to the rivers Hull and Humber. One of the remaining white iron cranes can be seen in the accompanying photograph. To these quiet waters, Humber keels once carried flour and agricultural products, taking back coal and linseed. The corn mill set up for the Driffield and East Riding Pure Linseed Cake Company has been turned into flats. A flourishing seed and grain business is still conducted by the Mortimer family. John Robert Mortimer (1825-1911), born at Fimber, ten miles (16km) to the west, was

once a miller here, but his fame rests as a distinguished amateur archaeologist and author of *Forty Years' Research in British and Saxon Burial Grounds of East Yorkshire.*

Despite competition from the Hull and Bridlington Railway after 1845, the canal survived commercially for another century. Nowadays, Riverhead is a scene of pleasure-boating and sailing.

Site: Riverhead is situated immediately behind Driffield railway station.

Grid Ref: TA 028568 (Market Weighton, Landranger 106)

A Family Tree Tomb

Immediately to the left as you enter Lowthorpe Church's south door is this bizarre and altogether remarkable tomb, believed to date from the fourteenth century. It shows a man and woman dressed in flowing robes, lying under a wispy coverlet, with a tree growing horizontally over it. From the network of branches sprout thirteen children's heads, seven on the man's side, six on the woman's. This arrestingly graphic tomb top probably represents the family of Sir John Heslerton of nearby Ruston Parva, who founded a chantry in 1364 to commend them all to their maker.

At the back, and separate, is a roughly-carved pre-Norman stone crosshead.

Site: Lowthorpe Church is reached by a minor road branching south off the A166, four miles north-east of Driffield.

Grid Ref: TA 079608 (Scarborough & Bridlington, Landranger 101)

Wells of Legend

As an object of reverence and pilgrimage, St John's Well in Harpham is entitled to the high degree of protection shown in the photograph. Annually in spring, local children place primroses on St John's tomb in Beverley Minister; and a patronal service involves worshippers in a walk from the church to this well. For Harpham is the historic birthplace of St John of Beverley (c640-721), once Bishop of Hexham and York, and founder of a church community that preceded Beverley Minster. The large, round stone always seems to have water sparkling at its base from the nearby spring. Some folk have invested this water with curative properties.

The other well, Drummer's, situated near the tennis courts behind the church, is associated with a curse. Centuries ago, whilst his men were busy at their archery practice, Lord St Quintin accidentally knocked the drummer boy into the well. The mother swore that whenever a future St Quintin was about to die, drumbeats from the well would be heard. But nowadays the St Quintins have departed from the village, though their memorials are numerous in a side chapel.

At Huggate, six miles (9.5km) north-east of Pocklington, the well on the green is said to be the deepest in England at 339 feet (103m).

Site: East End, Harpham. The village is just south of the A166 road, five miles (8km) north-east of Driffield.

Grid Ref: TA 095617 (Scarborough & Bridlington, Landranger 101)

Flood Prone in the High Wolds

Freak storms have several times devastated the North Wolds village of Langtoft. Two 'Great Floods', more than 200 years apart, are commemorated on the same notice. A few yards further down Back Street another plaque, on East Villa, records the height of the 1892 waters at the six foot (2m) level.

But there have been a number of lesser deluges. During a thunderstorm in May 1853, three horses were struck by lightning and ploughs were destroyed. In June 1888 a waterspout burst over the village, washing down mud and boulders, and carrying off household goods as it swept in at back doors and out at the front. No wonder the village green is known as the Pond! We may also muse over the name of the Ship Inn, so far inland!

The villagers had one thing to be grateful for on the 24th July 1912 — they escaped the floodwaters that brought out boats and bathers in the streets of Beverley and neighbouring villages.

Site: Corner House, Back Street, Langtoft; the village is on the B1249, seven miles north of Driffield.

Grid Ref: TA 011669 (Scarborough & Bridlington, Landranger 101)

A Norman Manor House

Surviving secular Norman buildings are quite rare. This ancient manor house, erected in Burton Agnes about 1170 by Roger de Stuteville, was occupied by local lords prior to the building of the Jacobean hall next door. The later brick facing was added about 1605, to be in keeping with the splendid new hall.

The undercroft, pictured below, is supported by five rounded central pillars, and the admirable vaulted arches have been well-maintained. The floor consists of rough brickwork. Sash windows were added during the eighteenth century. Up to 1610 the undercroft was used for storage and servants' quarters.

In the north-west corner, a winding stair leads to the upper storey. This much-modified room provided accommodation for the lord and his retainers. Other buildings — chapel, kitchen and stables — have long disappeared.

Behind the house is a donkey tread-wheel, twelve feet (3.5m) in diameter, and sturdy enough for younger visitors to try out.

The old manor house is maintained by the Department of the Environment.

Site: Burton Agnes, immediately west of the stately hall. The village is on the A166 road from Driffield to Bridlington.

Grid Ref: TA 103633 (Scarborough & Bridlington, Landranger 101)

Gatehouse To A Stately Home

Burton Agnes Hall was designed by Robert Smithson, Queen Elizabeth's master mason, who was the architect also of Longleat and Hardwick Hall. It was built between 1600 and 1610 for Sir Henry Griffith (1559-1620) whose descendants, the Boynton family, still live there.

The gatehouse is a satisfyingly beautiful structure, symmetrically arranged, its corner turrets ogee-capped, and its central focus the arms of King James I, flanked by female figures. The archway prepares the visitor for the varied splendours and curiosities of a magnificent Jacobean stately home, with a long gallery of paintings to rival any in the land.

Once the hall had a ghost. On her deathbed Lady Ann Griffith, daughter of the founder, asked for her head to be buried inside her lovely house, and returned to haunt it until her request was eventually granted.

Site: Burton Agnes is on the A166, midway between Driffield and Bridlington. In the village the hall is well signposted. It is open to the public from April to October and a charge is made for admission.

Grid Ref: TA 104633 (Scarborough and Bridlington, Landranger 101)

A Latin Treasure Hunt

The road boundaries to Wold House Farm are unique for their pairs of bell-shaped concrete blocks with cryptic Latin inscriptions. During the 1960s the farmer, Mr Newark Andrews, marked the numerous entrances to his fields with these huge bells, partly to commemorate old field-names originating with the enclosure movement. West from the farm along the A166, for instance, we may find '*Lingua Maxima*' (Big Tongue). And this, the old Roman road to York is acknowl-edged by '*Eboracum Via XX*'.

But this trail produces also much humour, and occasional advertising. By the Millington turning, for instance, a block (instead of a bell) reads 'Petrol Six Furlongs *Hic Opus Est*'.

Along the parallel North Wolds Walk is '*Aditus* Huggate'; and by the signpost at the south-east corner of the estate we find '*Vallis* Watermanhole *Magna*' -- and in one or two places simply 'Keep Britain Tidy'!

Mr Andrews was an original, a companionable man, good-humoured and widely respected across these glorious Wolds. His bells are a delightful legacy, and tracking them down is a fulfilling and rewarding exercise.

Site: Fridaythorpe parish. The roughly rectangular boundaries of Wold House Farm extend westwards along the A166; briefly down the Millington road, turning east again along the North Wolds Walk; and north back to the farm.

Grid Ref: SE 856576 (Market Weighton, Landranger 106)

A Divided Priory

Visitors to St Mary's Church have but to walk through the back of the churchyard to find the grassy mounds of the ancient priory, founded c1150 by Eustace Fitzjohn, a powerful Anglo-Norman baron. It was of the order of Gilbert of Sempringham, a foundation unusual in that it accommodated both monks and nuns, albeit separately, under one roof.

Watton, then, was a large 'double house', the biggest of its kind in England, six hundred feet (182m) long. The west part was for the nuns, the east for the monks. The two communities were kept strictly apart, sharing only a dividing wall between them even for corporate mass. Although the priory was dissolved by Henry VIII in 1539, the fifteenth-century prior's house has survived as a private dwelling, and is known as Watton Priory. Some parts hidden from view, like the vaulted undercroft, date from the fourteenth century. The centrepiece is this five-sided stone bay, flanked by castellated turrets, not quite matching, of Tudor brick. To the right the porch is Victorian.

Site: Watton Priory is some six miles (9.5km) south of Driffield, just off the A164, and behind the parish church.

Grid Ref: TA 027497 (Kingston upon Hull, Landranger 107)

T' Awd Squire

The Sykes Monument, a splendid 120 foot (36m) look-out tower near Sledmere, was built in 1865 in honour of Sir Tatton Sykes (1771-1863), fourth baronet of Sledmere, by tenants 'who loved him as a friend and honoured him as a landlord'. Sculptured reliefs show Sir Tatton on horseback and in various activities about his estate.

During his lifetime it was claimed that in his long frock-coat, high boots and breeches, white neck-cloth and frilled shirt, Sir Tatton was, with York Minster and Fountains Abbey, one of the three great sights of Yorkshire. A redoubtable barefist scrapper who spoke in local dialect to friends of all social classes, Sir Tatton founded the famous Sledmere stud farm, encouraged the use of bonemeal fertiliser, built several village schools and restored a number of Wolds churches —which last interest was enthusiastically developed by his son, another Sir Tatton.

The monument is surrounded by a ha-ha, a wall set in a ditch creating a kind of moat, but allowing full view.

Site: Garton Hill, south-east of Sledmere on the B1252.

Grid Ref: SE 958617 (Scarborough & Bridlington, Landranger 101)

The Waggoners' Memorial

Commissioned by Sir Mark Sykes and sculpted in Portland stone by A Barr, the estate mason, and Carlo Magnoni, this twenty foot (6m) high memorial was erected at Sledmere in 1919 as a tribute to the 1200 horse drivers recruited to the Service Corps in the early years of World War One. In some cases Sir Mark had withdrawn them literally straight from the fields.

His estimation of their usefulness and valour on the battlefields of France was abundantly justified. Various phases are shown clearly on the monument, eg driving competitions to encourage recruitment; waggoners receiving their call-up papers; embarkation for France; enemy cruelty and pillage. Across the road in Sledmere Church, an illuminated book of remembrance may be consulted.

Nearby, in imitation of the Eleanor Crosses, is a sixty foot (18m) high Gothic stone erected in 1900, and subsequently adapted as a war memorial.

Site: wooded roadside, Main Street, western fringe of Sledmere, on the B1252. The village is situated about eight miles (13km) north-west of Driffield.

Grid Ref: SE 928647 (Scarborough & Bridlington, Landranger 101)

Stamford Bridge and the North Wolds

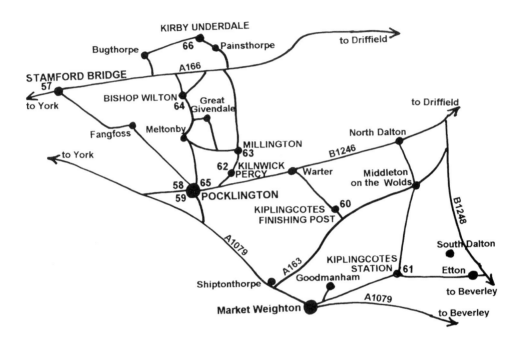

57. Battle of Stamford Bridge memorial
58. The flying man's memorial, Pocklington
59. Penny Arcadia, Pocklington
60. Kiplingcotes winning post
61. Kiplingcotes station
62. Buddhist centre, Kilnwick Percy
63. Unusual ceiling map, Gate Inn, Millington
64. A beck bridge, Bishop Wilton
65. Burnby Hall Gardens, Pocklington
66. Harold's Chair, Kirby Underdale

The Last Saxon Victory

A bronze plaque on a sandstone boulder commemorates simply the epic battle fought near here on the 25th September 1066. Harold, the last Saxon king, defeated his envious and treacherous half-brother Tostig, who, supported by Harold Hardrada of Norway and a huge Viking force of 60,000 men, had sailed up the Humber and captured York. Another reminder of the conflict is the sign on the Swordsman Inn in Stamford Bridge, showing a giant Viking being speared underneath the vital bridge. For hours, says the legend, this formidable enemy had contemptuously repulsed all attacks, until two Saxons paddled a boat to strike at him from below.

Harold's time to savour the ensuing victory was short. A few weeks later his army had to march to the south coast to do battle with invaders from France and, at Hastings, William of Normandy became the Conqueror.

Site: Stamford Bridge, just below the corn mill and on the bank of the River Derwent, alongside the A166.

Grid Ref: SE 713556 (Market Weighton, Landranger 106)

A Trapeze Wizard's Come-Uppance?

Thomas Pelling was undoubtedly a daring and adroit travelling showman who enjoyed thrilling and teasing his earthbound audiences. As the memorial shows, this 'flying man' was killed when he lost his balance and fell off a rope suspended between a pinnacle on Pocklington church tower and the roof of the neighbouring Old Star Inn. His batman-style dress, supported by stiffened wings attached to his arms and legs, had hitherto charmed and reassured the crowds — and perhaps himself. But on this occasion, the 10th April 1733, he came to grief, and a few days later was buried where he had fallen.

Pocklington had already known other unusual deaths, several for witchcraft allegations. One was the infamous case of Old Wife Green who in 1630 had been lynched and burnt in the market place for possessing the evil eye.

Site: Pocklington churchyard. The memorial is by the east window.

Grid Ref: SE 803490 (Market Weighton, Landranger 106)

What The Butler Saw

Penny Arcadia in Pocklington houses a comprehensive collection, possibly the world's largest, of coin-operated amusements. Some American items are over 100 years old and more than 100 machines are demonstrated. The variety is impressive: musical, gambling, fortune-telling, pin-tables, strength tests and viewers, for example.

Has the young lady in the photograph been surprised by what she has seen? Time was when people were shocked by the Can-can, but parties of school children, long inured to adult entertainment on modern video and television, will find the Arcadia colourful but innocent. Apart from all the mechanical marvels, magic mirrors etc, the performance includes a dance organ, a revolving stage and a screen show tracing the history of popular entertainment.

Site: Market Place, Pocklington.

Grid Ref: SE 804490 (Market Weighton, Landranger 106)

England's Oldest Horse Race?

According to the winning post's inscription, the Kiplingcotes Derby is the oldest horse race in the kingdom, going back to 1519. The first authentic account, supported by York diocesan records, confirms that there were horse races in this area in 1555; but the date widely accepted is 1618 when Lord Burlington, assisted by five noblemen, nineteen baronets and twenty-five gentlemen of Yorkshire, properly organised the race.

On the third Thursday in March, between 12 noon and 2pm, the four mile (6.4km) race is run over a rough course starting near the old Kiplingcotes Station and finishing at this winning post. It is an open race, women having been eligible since 1933. But every jockey's weight must be adjusted to ten stone (63.5kg), if necessary by carrying flints. Competitors must weigh in at the finishing post before 11am, where a considerable crowd gathers whatever the weather. The winner takes the interest from the original fund, roughly £20 nowadays. Second takes £4 from every entrant's fee, thus often bettering the winner. The clerk of the course is also the judge, a position which tends to be held in the same family for many years.

Site: the Kiplingcotes winning post is situated a quarter of a mile up the Warter road, north of the A163 between Market Weighton and Middleton on the Wolds.

Grid Ref: SE 895476 (Market Weighton, Landranger 106)

Tracking the Railway King

The old Kiplingcotes Station makes a convenient stopping point along the Hudson Way, from Market Weighton to Beverley; or as a worthwhile visit by road. This track was part of the York—Hull grand design of George Hudson, the East Riding entrepreneur who became known as the Railway King. Thrice Lord Mayor of York, Hudson misappropriated railway funds, fled to France, was imprisoned at York and is buried in Scrayingham churchyard.

This part of the line was completed in 1865 by the North-Eastern Railway, which took over after Hudson's fall from power. Curiously, it closed exactly a century later under the Beeching plan to axe uneconomic services. The station house remains, converted to a refreshments room, with an antiques sales room a few yards away. Along the platform opposite are displayed various former domestic artefacts and farm implements. To the west is a chalk quarry, a Site of Special Scientific Interest.

Site: Kiplingcotes Station is some 3¹/₂ miles (5.5km) north-east of Market Weighton. It can be reached by walking along the dismantled line, or by minor roads linking with Etton, Middleton on the Wolds and Market Weighton.

Grid Ref: SE 929439 (Market Weighton, Landranger 106)

A Buddhist Manor House

Eight unfluted columns support this enormous Ionic portico, the architectural focus of Kilnwick Percy's sylvan stately mansion. It was built in 1845 as the manor house, beautifully positioned between two lakes in attractive parkland. This rural retreat is assuredly one of the most scenically favoured in this Riding, reminding one of sites sought by medieval monks.

Since 1979 the house has become the Madhyamaka Buddhist Centre. Day and residential classes are offered on such themes as mind/body harmony and 'happy mind, happy life'. Visitors are most welcome. It is hard to think of natural surroundings better calculated to assist meditation.

Site: Kilnwick Percy is some 1½ miles (2.5km) east of Pocklington off the B1246.

Grid Ref: SE 825499 (Market Weighton, Landranger 106)

A Ceiling Scenario

The Gate Inn at Millington recalls the localised word 'gait', a unit of land capable of providing pasturage for six sheep. Under the Enclosure Acts the parish was divided into 108 such gaits. But this fascinating old pub has a more tangible geographical oddity — a huge map of Yorkshire painted right across the bar-room ceiling. Commissioned about 1970 by Alan Moore, a former landlord, it is said to be best appreciated from a recumbent posture!

By the farm entrance a few yards up the main street, a wheel is set into the pavement. It was a hooping iron used by the smith to shape the iron rims of cart wheels. Few are left, though they were once a common sight. Until his skills were replaced by the tractor revolution, the blacksmith was called on not only for shoeing but for repairs to farm implements and domestic and ornamental ironwork. Here then is one old tool of the trade that has itself become a museum piece, an ornament and an oddity.

Site: The Gate Inn, Millington. The village is about four miles (6.5km) north-east of Pocklington, reached by minor roads.

Grid Ref: SE 831516 (Market Weighton, Landranger 106)

A Much-Bridged Beck

Attractive becks (Danish for brooks) are commonplace in the East Riding, but Bishop Wilton's has cut deeply and widely. The resultant grassy vale is criss-crossed by bridges giving access to cottages and houses on either bank. By the main bridge near the Fleece Inn, shepherds and farmers once damned the beck to make a wash dyke for cleaning the sheep in summer. Opposite the church gates, a flight of steps has been built to help pedestrians to cross from one side of the beck to the other.

St Edith's Church is worth visiting. Every square foot of the floor of the nave is patterned with a black and white mosaic of such birds as lapwing, duck and magpie.

Far back in 1086, 'Wiltone' was described in *Domesday Book* as a 'wild and uncultivated enclosure of farmsteads'. At the top end of the beck, the humps and hollows of Archbishop Neville's medieval palace may still be seen opposite the school. From here the road climbs to Garrowby Hill, 800 feet (243m) above sea level, the highest point in the Riding.

Site: Bishop Wilton is about five miles (8km) north of Pocklington.

Grid Ref: SE 798553 (Market Weighton, Landranger 106)

Stewart's Kingdom

These eight acres (3ha) of exotically landscaped gardens were the creation of Major Percy Stewart (1871-1962), who enjoyed a lively career as a soldier, schoolmaster, big game hunter, writer and landscape artist. His work at Burnby Hall, which he bought in 1904, continued over many years, particularly after his extensive travelling days were done and he returned to Pocklington. He had immense energy and catholic interests, fed by world-wide experiences and contacts. The two lakes, built at different levels, he constructed largely by himself. They hold the finest collection of water lilies in Europe, more than fifty varieties, and are very well stocked with roach, mirror and koi carp, and goldfish. There are 1,100 rose bushes and many ranges of holly, heather and dwarf conifers.

Inside the museum, mounted exhibits include Mexican sharks, Australian giant eels, a Rhodesian lioness, together with African and Javan musical instruments, religious artefacts from Burma and Tibet, and many unusual figure sculptures rarely seen elsewhere.

Site: Burnby Hall Gardens, Pocklington, are set in the south-east corner of the town by the B1247.

Grid Ref: SE 806485 (Market Weighton, Landranger 106)

Sermons In Stone

Some curious stones are on view in this churchyard of All Saints at Kirby Underdale, which, unusually, lies in a hollow, reached by twenty-four descending stone steps! Set in the grass near the south porch is this stone chair known hereabouts as Harold's Chair, though Harold is difficult to identify. Unearthed on Garrowby Hill (the highest point in the Riding), it is believed to be the former square base of a medieval parish boundary stone.

To the left of the porch lies an old limestone coffin, removed from the church precincts about 1870 and used for many years as a cattle trough. Inside the porch is the much-travelled tombstone of Roger Wilberfoss (1532) of Garrowby.

Visitors may enjoy the hunt for a small and elusive merrill square, three concentric squares arranged around a central hole. It is located east of the porch, in the angle of the wall above four flat gravestones and about one yard (1m) up from the gravel. Merrill was nine men's morris, played with counters rather like noughts and crosses. Never quite dying out in Yorkshire, the game is being revived again, for example, at Hutton le Hole, North Yorkshire, where championships are held.

Finally, round the back of the church is the impressive burial ground of the Halifax family, several stones adorned with a metal family crest.

Site: All Saints Church, Kirby Underdale, is eleven miles (17.5km) north-east of Stamford Bridge, off the A166.

Grid Ref: SE 808586 (Market Weighton, Landranger 106)

The Market Weighton Area

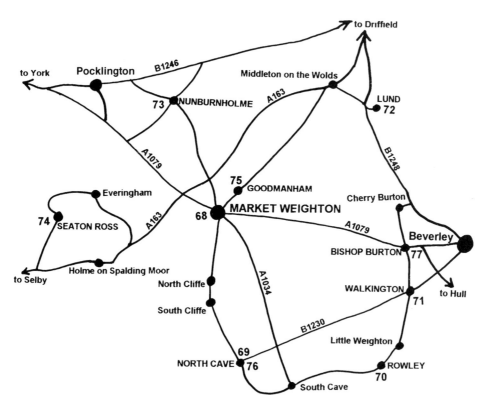

68. Bradley's footprint, Market Weighton
69. Ypres casualty board, North Cave
70. Croquet green and church, Rowley
71. House with church architecture, Walkington
72. Forge to bus shelter, Lund

73. Anglo-Saxon cross, Nunburnholme
74. Dial Hall Farm, Seaton Ross
75. Commemorative cross, Goodmanham
76. Dovecote, North Cave
77. The Altisidora, Bishop Burton

Giant Footsteps

Born into a very large family at Market Weighton in 1787, William Bradley became England's tallest man. Weighing a stone (6.3kg) at birth, he had attained twenty-seven stone (171.5kg) when he died in 1820, and his height was 7 feet 9 inches (2.35m). His stockings were said to be nearly four feet (1.2m) long and his walking stick taller than the average man. His boots were specially made. In the Bradley Room of the Londesborough Arms Hotel, near a picture of the great man and a friend, is a replica of the sole of his boot made by John Walker of Hull. Just up the road, opposite the market, is Bradley House, specially built for him, and displaying another foot plaque measuring 15 inches (38cm) in length and 6 inches (15cm) across the sole.

Travelling about the country, William made a good living as a fairground freak. King George III was so impressed by his stature and good manners that he gave him a gold chain as a souvenir. Oddly, William was said to be only a moderate eater and he died early of consumption. In order to deter body-snatchers he was buried secretly at night, but he was later re-interred inside All Saints Church, just to the right of the tower arch, where there is a notice to his memory.

Site: Bradley House is by the market place on the York road (A1079) at Market Weighton.

Grid Ref: SE 876418 (Market Weighton, Landranger 106)

Lest We Forget

At this lovely corner of North Cave where an old church, a busy stream and parkland converge, we find on the wall of Hotham Hall Lodge these devastating statistics of the carnage of war. These casualty figures of the Battle of Ypres in World War One are calculated to stop us in our tracks. They are a very direct reminder of the cost in human lives of defending that notorious salient, reading almost like a quotation from *Oh What a Lovely War*. Like that celebrated show, the message should divert our thoughts for a while to reflection and wonder. The noticeboard was erected shortly after the war by the late Colonel T C Clitheroe DSO of Hotham Hall.

Site: Hotham Hall Lodge, Church Lane, North Cave.

Grid Ref: SE 896328 (Market Weighton, Landranger 106)

The Rowley Exodus

In fine weather, croquet is played any day of the week on this beautiful green adjoining Rowley Church. But it would not have been allowed on a Sunday during the rectorship (1621-38) of the Rev Ezekiel Rogers. Church of England incumbents were then required to proclaim the Book of Sports which permitted games to be played after Sunday morning services. But Ezekiel's conscience was disturbed, and after persistently refusing to read from 'that accursed book', he was suspended from his Rowley living by Archbishop Laud.

   The parson's puritanical mind then took a new turn. He decided to leave for America, and eventually led some thirty families from Rowley and neighbouring villages to found a new community (eventually called Rowley) in the state of Massachusetts. Many American visitors come here to the manor — ironically a former rectory, though not in Ezekiel's time — to see the church where the protests began.

Site: Rowley Manor and Church of St Peter are ¾ mile (1.2km) south-west of Little Weighton.

Grid Ref: SE 975326 (Market Weighton, Landranger 106)

Enterprising Walkington

Many East Riding villages show unusual combinations of brick and stone where repairs have been made. But at Walkington an imaginative and innovative family of builders has, over several generations, made a distinctive contribution to domestic architectural styles. Relics from redundant places of worship have been incorporated in a number of village houses, not all of them of great antiquity. Here, at 48 West End (c1895), we have a considerable 'chapel front' extension, left, flanked in the garden, right, by a piece of masonry that probably once stood at a higher level on a church.

Walkington has a fine community spirit, and a reputation for doing things. It has its own song, always sung after the seasonal pantomime. Since 1967, on the third Sunday in June, a recreated Victorian hayride, with horse-drawn wagons, carriages and suitably-costumed villagers, has paraded to neighbouring Bishop Burton and Beverley, raising thousands of pounds for charity.

Site: 48 West End, Main Street, Walkington. The village is on the B1230 some three miles (5km) west of Beverley.

Grid Ref: SE 996370 (Market Weighton, Landranger 106)

From Blacksmith's To Bus Shelter

At first sight this bus shelter at Lund seems not particularly noteworthy, save for the plaque drawing attention to the village's award-winning successes in Yorkshire competitions. Closer attention, however, shows that here was the former black-smith's hearth. To left and right the basic heavier artefacts have been preserved and incorporated in this building, which was modified in 1970.

In the East Riding, as elsewhere, the coming of the tractor has virtually eliminated the need for horses — although they are still used at Hasholme Farm near Holme-on-Spalding-Moor, where exhibitions are still held.

Some other forges have been interestingly revamped. At Burton Pidsea, near Withernsea, the Nancy Inn retains its anvil and fireplace, and is readily viewed from the bar; and at Laxton, by the Humber, a farrier's workshop still fashions wrought-iron work, and many of the old tools are there to see.

Site: the bus shelter is in front of All Saints Church, Lund. The village lies on the B1248 road, six miles (9.5km) north-west of Beverley.

Grid Ref: SE 971482 (Market Weighton, Landranger 106)

A Cross — Christian and Pagan

Two unusual circumstances make Nunburnholme Church a place of pilgrimage. Inside, at the west end stand these two sections (a third is missing) of the shaft of an Anglo-Saxon cross, from around AD 1000. Rediscovered in the walls during a restoration of 1872, it incorporates a mixture of sculptural styles and artistic ideas, but unmistakable are a Viking warrior on the east face, and the Virgin and Child on the west face. Other motifs include carvings of animals — a lamb, a dragon, a centaur. Was the original intention some synthesis of Christian and pagan worlds, perhaps?

Outside, buried near the south door are two distinguished former incumbents, father and son. The Rev Francis Orpen Morris, rector from 1854 to 1893, was a renowned ornithologist and antiquary who produced six volumes of *A Natural History of British Birds*. The Rev Marmaduke Charles Francis Morris, who followed as rector until 1910, was an expert on dialect and customs, and author of the standard work, *Yorkshire Folk Talk*, in 1892.

Site: St James' Church, Nunburnholme, is seven miles (11km) north-west of Market Weighton.

Grid Ref: SE 847478 (Market Weighton, Landranger 106)

Sundial Village

After a century and a half, the stories told about William Watson (1784-1857) have passed into legend and hearsay. What is beyond doubt is the evidence left of his grand passion — sundials, enormous ones, as big as a house!

Farmer and surveyor, he lived at Dial Hall Farm, just outside the village of Seaton Ross. Painted across the front is this giant sundial, with a twelve foot (3.6m) diameter. A similar one is on a cottage at North End in the village. They were created about 1840. Watson, an obsessive timekeeper, wanted to shame some of his young farm lads into leaving their beds earlier of a morning. His grandiose gestures have been well preserved.

Above the south door of St Edmund's Church is another of William's sundials, this time of a modest scale. It is recalled in his epitaph, the second gravestone on the right by the churchyard gate:

'At this church I so often with pleasure did call,
that I made a sundial upon the church wall.'

Site: Melbourne Road, Seaton Ross. The village is about five miles (8km) north-west of Holme-on-Spalding Moor and can be reached via the A163 and minor roads; or by leaving the A1079 York-Beverley road at Hayton.

Grid Ref: SE 774426 (Market Weighton, Landranger 106)

'This One Time Place of Idols'

In the middle of Goodmanham churchyard, a wooden cross erected on a stone base from Londesborough Hall marks the spot where Archbishop Cosmo Gordon of York stood on the 21st July 1927 to commemorate the cradling of Christianity in this part of Yorkshire.

Thirteen hundred years earlier Edwin, King of Northumbria, had been converted by the missionary Paulinus, brought from Kent by the new Queen, Ethelburga, herself a recent convert. The historian Bede, in circa AD 731, told of a change of heart by the high priest, Coifi, an uncompromising pagan until he came under the spell of Paulinus at a council held at nearby Londesborough. Riding straight from this meeting, Coifi stormed into his own temple, hurled spears at its image and set fire to it. From the ashes there arose a Christian church, and it is believed that the present building of All Saints (c1130) stands on the same site.

Inside, a chancel plaque records the 1927 commemoration service; and stained glass windows portray Edwin, Ethelburga, Coifi brandishing a flaming torch, and Bede, from whose description our title is drawn.

Site: Goodmanham churchyard, 1½ miles (2.5km) north-east of Market Weighton, is reached by a minor road.

Grid Ref: SE 889432 (Market Weighton, Landranger 106)

When Doves Were Loved

The right to keep doves was once the lordly privilege of landowners and monasteries, and was not extended to commoners until 1613. In medieval times the birds were valuable for fresh meat during winter and, of course, for fresh eggs. Their dung could be used as manure and even in the manufacture of gunpowder. But as agricultural improvements made animal foodstuffs more plentiful, enabling livestock to be kept throughout the winter, pigeons lost their appeal.

Although sometimes found on older farms into the twentieth century, dovecotes have become rarer in the English countryside. In the East Riding there remains, for example, the Dovecote, with additional garden boxes, at Bessingby. Another has been restored next to the George and Dragon at Holmpton. Our photograph is of the charming late eighteenth century dovecote at Manor Farm, North Cave. This octagonal stone building has a slate roof, crowned by a decorated cupola. Pairs of nesting boxes are still arranged around the inside.

Site: Manor Farm, North Cave, is next door to the parish church on the B1230 road from Newport to Beverley.

Grid Ref: SE 897327 (Market Weighton, Landranger 106)

Turf Winners

A popular venue in this picture postcard village of Bishop Burton is the Altisidora Inn, a building of considerable antiquity, previously known as Evander and later as the Horse and Jockey. The change to Altisidora came in 1813 when the horse of that name, owned by the lord of the manor, Richard Watt, won the St Leger. An experienced breeder and trainer, Watt won the race again in 1830 with Rockingham, his other horse, Belshezzar, coming second. Rockingham's name survives on the hostelry at Lockington, off the A164 north of Beverley.

At Burton Pidsea, six miles (9.6km) north-west of Withernsea, the Nancy Inn commemorates the horse that in 1851 won twelve out of thirteen races, including the Chester Cup. Interestingly, the horse was stabled at the Rose and Crown, Beverley, closely adjacent to the racecourse which is passed on the way to Bishop Burton.

Site: the Altisidora is a prominent building on the A1079 at Bishop Burton, three miles (5km) west of Beverley.

Grid Ref: SE 992398 (Market Weighton, Landranger 106)

Goole and the South-West

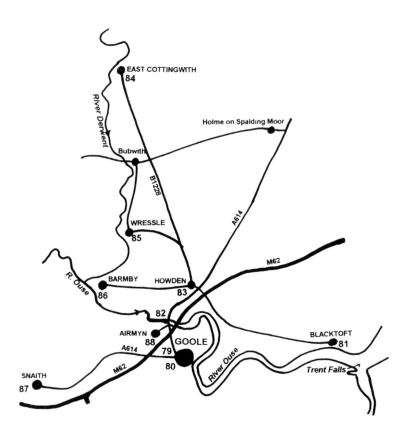

79. Viking ship and swans logo, Goole
80. No 5 Boat Hoist, Goole
81. Blacktoft Jetty
82. Boothferry Bridge
83. Fruit house, Howden
84. Snowden Slight's grave, East Cottingwith
85. Wressle Castle
86. Barmby tidal barrage
87. Penny cells, Snaith
88. Airmyn clock tower

Vikings and Swans

Goole's charter of incorporation was presented by the HRH Prince George, the future King George VI, on the 27th October 1933. Intriguingly, a Viking ship and three swans are shown on the approved coat-of-arms. The Viking link may seem a bit tenuous, as there was little development of this small settlement until the nineteenth century. True, Goole did develop as a port, and its location was incontrovertibly in the ancient Danelaw! The three swans are more satisfactorily explained, for in times past Goole paid *spiritualia* or dues to Selby Abbey, whose own arms included swans.

This huge logo is displayed above the main entrance to the town's 1896 market hall. To left and right, the motif of ship and swans is repeated in a line of titles. Below, on the glass doors of the entrance, the design has been adapted in a freer fashion.

Site: Goole town centre.

Grid Ref: SE 746236 (Market Weighton, Landranger 106)

No 5 Boat Hoist

From 1862 until 1986, coal was brought to Goole by canal from the West Riding in 'trains' of square containers called pans or 'Tom Puddings' (they wobbled!). This system was devised by the distinguished Victorian engineer to the Aire and Calder Navigation Company, William Hammond Bartholomew (1830-1919). On arrival, each pan was raised by a hydraulic hoist and its forty tons were shot direct down a chute into the hold of a waiting ship. No 5 Boat Hoist pictured here, built in 1912 by W G Armstrong and based on Bartholomew's earlier designs, survives as a listed building in South Dock.

Close by is the Sobriety Waterside Centre which displays material on 'Bartholomew's Vineyard', as Goole's complex of docks and canals became known. Two remaining Tom Puddings are generally moored here and may be inspected.

Site: South Dock, Goole, is situated between Albert Street and the Dutch River. It can be reached either via Stanhope Street from the town centre, or via the A161 to Old Goole.

Grid Ref: SE 734225 (Market Weighton, Landranger 106)

Blacktoft Jetty

West of neighbouring Faxfleet, which looks across these waters to Trent Falls, the river's name changes from Humber to Ouse. Changing, too, are the tides, so much so that cargo ships plying between Goole and Hull sometimes have to lay by at Blacktoft until the rising waters enable them to continue. This concrete jetty, administered by Associated British Ports, was built in 1956, replacing a decaying wooden structure from Victorian times.

Vessels from many European countries, particularly from the Baltic area, dock here for a few hours, though cargoes are not unloaded. Our photograph happens to be of a Turkish ship transferring a load of steel from Goole to Hull. Often the crews have long enough to walk along the short embankment to the Hope and Anchor Inn, or go for a stroll through this quiet village which otherwise seems far removed from continental influences. Some other migrants are occasionally noisy, for just downstream at Blacktoft Sand there is an RSPB Nature Reserve.

Site: Blacktoft Jetty is situated on the River Ouse, six miles (9.5km) east of Goole.

Grid Ref: SE 844242 (Market Weighton, Landranger 106)

Boothferry Bridge

'Boothferry' derives its name from the ancient ferry service which had operated at Booth, a hamlet to the west of this bridge built in 1929 by the Cleveland Bridge and Engineering Company.

This multi-span steel lattice girder structure was designed with a moveable section at its northern end to allow shipping access to Selby and the Humber. In its

prime days the bridge was regarded as a novel engineering feat, and a vital link between the west of the county and Hull and the east coast. But by the late 1960s its two narrow lanes were carrying over 30,000 vehicles a day; and in 1975 the Ouse Bridge, a flyover to link with the M62, was constructed less than half a mile (0.8km) downstream. These contrasting bridges lend new dimensions to an otherwise flat and muddy terrain. Nowadays, Boothferry Bridge is used mainly by non-motorway traffic, pedestrians and cyclists.

Site: Boothferry, where the A614 crosses the River Ouse. Strictly speaking the bridge falls within the parish of Airmyn.

Grid Ref: SE 734264 (Market Weighton, Landranger 106)

The Fruit House

Here, within the shadow of Howden Minster, is this peculiar, castellated little house built directly over a winding brook near the picturesque Ashes Playing Field. Centuries ago it stood in the middle of a large orchard. Surprisingly, it was a two-storey building, with the upper room, brick-built, used for storing fruit for the kitchen of the nearby Bishop's Palace, the summer residence of the Bishop of Durham.

During its restoration in 1927, medieval fragments from the Minster were embedded in the brickwork; the coped gable, for example, on the north side was decorated with bits of ancient tracery and the letters APF (Ashes Playing Field). In 1984 further restoration (eg a pantiled roof) was carried out by Howden Civic Society. A plaque on the north wall reads: 'On 9th October 1929 water used for the church fire was pumped from this moat near here being the only supply available'.

One hundred and fifty yards (135m) away, towards the Minster, stands the manor house, once part of the palace. Noteworthy is the corner porch, built by Walter Skirlaw, Bishop of Durham between 1388 and 1405.

Site: immediately south-east of Howden Minster, adjacent to the tennis courts en route to Ashes Playing Field. Enter at the corner of the market square.

Grid Ref: SE 748282 (Market Weighton, Landranger 106)

IN MEMORY OF
SNOWDEN SLIGHTS,
WILDFOWLER,
OF EAST COTTINGWITH,
BORN JUNE 14TH 1829,
DIED APRIL 15TH 1913.

That Notorious Wildfowler

In the churchyard at East Cottingwith, this unusual headstone of a duck in flight recalls the legendary wildfowler, Snowden Slights (1829-1913).

During his long professional lifetime, his name was a byword for the indiscriminate slaughter of ducks, geese, swans — anything that flew. A master of every aspect of his craft, Slights manoeuvred his fourteen foot (4.25m) punt skilfully over the waters, notably the flood-prone Wheldrake Ings nearby, using trees as cover, prepared to bide his time until the prey was near before opening up with the appropriate shotgun selected from his considerable armoury. His retriever dog was well trained to collect the birds, which Slights later distributed amongst his cronies —butchers, game dealers, blacksmiths, innkeepers and others who might do him return favours. Interestingly, Wheldrake Ings is now a Nature Reserve.

Site: East Cottingwith churchyard. The grave is in the south-west corner against a wall. The village lies some twelve miles (19km) north of Howden off the B1228.

Grid Ref: SE 704425 (Market Weighton, Landranger 106)

Wressle Castle

It was a fortified manor house, rather than a castle, and now the only one standing in the East Riding. Only the south side remains, the great hall and kitchens flanked by two unequal towers, whose walls are six feet (1.8m) thick at the base. At each corner of the original quadrangle stood a square tower, with a tower gatehouse on the north side opposite the great hall.

Wressle Castle was built about 1380 for Sir Henry Percy, Earl of Northumberland. There was much local support for the earl at the Battle of Otterburn in 1388, although the English were routed by Robert II. A later earl had not supported King Charles I during the Civil War; nevertheless, much of Wressle Castle was destroyed on the orders of Parliament. Fire damage in 1796 reduced the remainder to its present proportions.

Site: Wressle is about thee miles (5km) north-west of Howden, and the castle is set a little to the north of the railway crossing.

Grid Ref: SE 705316 (Market Weighton, Landranger 106)

Barmby Tidal Barrage

In 1972 this huge concrete barrier was built across the mouth of the River Derwent
to exclude the incoming tidal waters of the Ouse so that the high quality of Derwent
water could be maintained. Raw water is treated by Yorkshire Water a mile (1.5km)
upstream. Twin steel sluice-gates, each 23 feet (7m) long and 16½ feet (5m) deep,
their compartments encased in river mud, are automatically raised or lowered by
pulley action masterminded by a computer from the control box. On the far side
of the box is a lock also controlled by the site staff, permitting the passage of light
craft to and from the River Ouse. The National Rivers Authority, whilst allowing visitors
to walk across the concrete footway of the barrage, has taken precautions to prevent
accidents, and has attractively landscaped the adjacent greens and picnic sites.

Less than a mile away across the Ouse are the giant cooling towers of Drax Power
Station. In this frontier outpost where two traditional Ridings meet, man's efforts
to engineer and control his environment are spectacularly manifest.

*Site: the extreme west end of Barmby on the Marsh, at the junction of the Rivers
Ouse and Derwent. The village is about 3½ miles (5.5km) west of Howden, and is
reached via a minor road off the B1228, south of and parallel to the A63.*

Grid Ref: SE 679287 (Market Weighton, Landranger 106)

Penny Cells

Tradition insists that drunks, or their kind friends, had to pay one penny for their release when sober, a process sometimes hindered by other friends passing them further refreshment from outside. Hence the double sets of narrow grills in each window of this building in Snaith. Heavy wooden doors and windows were framed in stone, otherwise these three tiny cells were built of brick. Recent restoration includes pantile roofs. The block rates as a listed building of the eighteenth century, and is maintained by the Snaith and District Heritage Society.

Owing to the proximity of church and former market, there could have been several categories of offenders. Snaith had a peculiar, or church court, which might occasionally resort to shock treatment through public exposure. The market's charter dated from 1223, and its court might well consign dishonest traders to the cells, while fining them more than one penny, presumably.

Another lock-up, tiny and rounded, is at Workhouse Farm at Holme-on-Spalding-Moor, once used as a 'cooler' for erring workhouse inmates.

Site: Snaith Buttermarket, by the priory church of St Lawrence.

Grid Ref: SE 643223 (Market Weighton, Landranger 106)

A Tower Timely and Deserved

To mark the elevation of George Percy, lord of the manor and second Earl of Beverley to the title of Earl of Northumberland, this elegant clock tower at Airmyn was built by public subscription. On the south face is the simple inscription, 'George Earl of Beverley 1865'. At each corner, twelve feet (3.5m) above the turf, are plinths supporting a pair of shield-bearing angels. Below each angel is a triangle with a Yorkshire rose set in the middle. Other roses form a triangle around the two clock-faces, south and east. The clock keeps good time and strikes the hour.

Time has now brought many changes to this once small port on the tidal River Aire. Once the dead were carried by boat for burial at Snaith, lest floodwaters should cover local graves. The embankments have now been strengthened to prevent any possible flooding.

To the right of the clock tower is a private school originally founded as a Sunday school in 1834 by the same second earl, who was a considerable benefactor to this riverside community.

Site: High Street, Airmyn, two miles (3.2km) west of Goole.

Grid Ref: SE 725255 (Market Weighton, Landranger 106)

The Hessle Hinterland

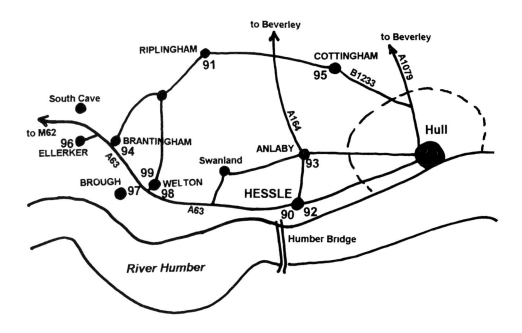

90. Humber Bridge Country Park
91. Riplingham airshafts
92. Cliff Mill, Hessle
93. Tranby Croft, Anlaby
94. Brantingham war memorial

95. Thompson's folly, Cottingham
96. Ellerker cottages
97. The Brough milestone
98. The Green Dragon, Welton
99. Cattle Well Spring, Welton

Nature's Country Park

For six centuries, chalk was quarried in this area of Hessle, which became known as Little Switzerland. As sections were progressively abandoned, they were quickly overgrown by foliage and shrub. With the opening of the Humber Bridge in 1981, the planning authorities had not far to look for an adjacent site offering ample parking facilities, walking and picnic areas, wildlife and leisure pursuits. Nature —

and generations of quarrymen —had virtually done the job. It remained for the county council to organise landscaping, footpaths, a nature trail, safety arrangements, and the recruitment of guides and maintenance staff. The result is a superb country park, very true to nature, with easy access, and all within the shadow of the Humber Bridge.

The park also offers many vantage points for viewing the bridge. One fascinating study in perspective is to walk under the anchorage behind the north tower, and then look up and around and across the river.

Site: The Humber Bridge Country Park is on Hessle Foreshore, behind the bridge. It can be reached via Heads Lane off the A53, Boothferry Road, Hessle.

Grid Ref: TA 022258 (Kingston upon Hull, Landranger 107)

The Wold That Smoked

Having left Little Weighton, where the former station continues as a private house, the Hull to Barnsley and West Riding line ran towards the Drewton Tunnel, 1 mile 354 yards (1,920m) long. Tales are still told of the doings of scores of navvies who lived rough in this rural countryside when the tunnel was excavated in the early 1880s. Five brick structures, rounded like small chimneys, were built in a line over these fields to serve as airshafts, dispersing the smoke that built up from the trains rushing through Drewton Tunnel. Up to the railway's closure in 1955, dwellers in rural Riplingham were accustomed to see billows of smoke drifting across these pastures.

Site: one and a half miles (2.5km) west of Little Weighton, the airshafts are visible near Riplingham Grange at the junction of minor roads to Beverley/South Cave and Newbald/ Welton.

Grid Ref: SE 964336 (Market Weighton, Landranger 106)

Cliff Mill

Chalk crushing was a considerable medieval industry in these southern wolds. Water was added to the powder, and the resultant slurry was dried off in settling pits and sheds. In later times the whiting was used in the manufacture of paints and putty.

Although a number of wind-powered whiting mills were built in the early nineteenth century, Cliff Mill, completed in 1825, is the only survivor. Its five roller-sails turned for exactly a hundred years, when the motive power was changed to gas. Until it was dwarfed by the mighty Humber Bridge, a stone's-throw away, this black brick tower was the dominant landmark on the foreshore. Some of the machinery remains and the mill has become its own museum. A number of old millstones may still be found on the site.

Site: Hessle Foreshore, close to the north tower of the Humber Bridge. It is reached via Heads Lane off the A53 Boothferry Road, Hessle.

Grid Ref: TA 023254 (Kingston upon Hull, Landranger 107)

The Baccarat Affair

Set in attractively landscaped grounds, Tranby Croft, on the western outskirts of Hull, was built and developed in the last quarter of the nineteenth century by the Wilson family, of shipping-line fame. Edward, Prince of Wales enjoyed his occasional visits, particularly when there seemed promise of a game or two of baccarat. His royal highness had learned the art in France, and generally brought his own counters to country-house weekends.

Unfortunately, on this occasion in September 1890 another friend, Sir William Gordon Cummings, lieutenant-colonel in the Scots Guards, was accused of cheating by manipulating the counters and adjusting his own stakes. Other players, embarrassed at first, resisted a confrontation; but after further complaints this guest was requested to leave, and was subsequently cashiered by the army. It was rumoured that Queen Victoria rebuked her heir for becoming involved, and suggested, without result, that he should take up bridge!

Site: Tranby Croft is on Tranby Lane, Anlaby. The premises, used by Hull Girls High School, are reached via the A63 from Hull, turning north onto the A164 Beverley Road for Anlaby.

Grid Ref: TA 023283 (Kingston upon Hull Landranger 107)

Estate Village With City Additions

Brantingham Dale is one of several valleys of the South Wolds whose well-wooded slopes rise steeply, reminiscent of the Derbyshire dales, and offering delightful walks and spectacular views. At the southern edge of the village, between pub and post office, is this war memorial, exceptional in that it was reconstructed from bits of Cuthbert Brodrick's Victorian town hall in Hull. Architecturally and aesthetically, it has always been controversial; but, lump it or like it, the visitor will own it is different. Other large flower urns around Brantingham are said to be from the same source.

Picturesque cottages, a duck pond and an old pump set in the middle of the road give way to a church beautifully sheltered on a lower slope of the Wold. Off a twisting and turning road, a choice of beaten tracks, including the Wolds Way, offer uphill-and-down-dale expeditions — or, for the more contemplative mind, glorious views over the River Humber and the Vale of York.

Site: Brantingham lies just off the A63 about nine miles (14.5km) west of Hull.
Grid Ref: SE 939295 (Market Weighton, Landranger 106)

Thompson's Folly

Partially sheltered by trees, this stone tower folly is all that remains of 'Cottingham Castle', once a mock-Gothic castellated mansion built in 1814-15 by a Hull banker and sometime MP, Thomas Thompson, who lived here until his death in 1828. Although he was chaffed by locals for the ostentation of his 'Castle', Thompson was generally well-respected and devised a successful scheme for making poor families self-sufficient on smallholdings in Cottingham.

Sadly, the castle was destroyed by fire in 1861, and the site was later cleared for the construction of Castle Hill Hospital. Thompson's castle is not, of course, to be confused with the village's historic Baynard Castle, which stood between Northgate and Hallgate, and of which little remains.

Site: the folly stands at the western fringe of Cottingham, near the roundabout at the junction of Castle Hill and the Hull-Beverley road (A164).

Grid Ref: TA 023322 (Kingston upon Hull, Landranger 107)

Curious Cottage Names

Several cottages in the pretty village of Ellerker have interesting histories. Here Sebastopol Cottage, delightfully situated by the beck at the edge of the green, has an unusual Gothic wall, built in 1857 by the master of Ellerker Hall. During the Crimean War he shipped guns to Russia, bringing back stone as ballast. Thinking that the lady at the cottage lacked privacy, he had this wall built for her from his supplies of imported stone. Hence the cottage's name.

Opposite is Blacksmith's Cottage, complete with black anvil. A few yards on is Pennyschool House, which was a dame's school during the latter part of the nineteenth century, charging a penny a week, like its rival, the National school on Howden Croft Hill, erected in 1845 and transformed into a commodious house. If you now turn up the alley to St Anne's Church, Amen Cottage stands to the right of the church gates. Here once lived the parish clerk, who loudly and dutifully added the 'so-be-it' word to the parson's prayers.

Site: Main Street, Ellerker. The village is reached via the A63, about ten miles (16km) west of Hull.

Grid Ref: SE 921295 (Market Weighton, Landranger 106)

Old Milestone, Old Route

Although milestones were used by the Romans, the idea lay dormant until the turnpike days of the eighteenth century. Local turnpike trusts were generally required to set up milestones at appropriate intervals, as well as to maintain a defined length of road by charging tolls.

This small wayside milestone marks the turnpike set up by Act of Parliament in 1771 to link Brough Ferry and North Newbald. As part of the old Ermine Street, this route had been developed by the Romans, who had built their town of Petuaria where Brough now stands. Restored in 1987 by Elloughton-cum-Brough Parish Council, this venerable stone still indicates to travellers and bystanders that York is thirty miles (48km) and Lincoln thirty-five miles (56km) away. This last distance may seem short — until one considers that for centuries the Humber was fordable; Brough to Lincoln via Boothferry or a bridge to the west would have added many miles to the journey.

Other interesting milestones are to be found at Milestone Farm, Westgate, North Cave; and outside Lund church; while outside the east end wall of Goodmanham church stands a cryptic modern one. Can you find it?

Site: Brough, outside the magistrates court at the junction of Station Road and Saltgrounds Road. Brough is about seven miles (11km) west of Hull, off the A63.

Grid Ref: SE 936266 (Market Weighton, Landranger 106)

DT's Pub

DT was, of course, Dick Turpin, and it was here at the Green Dragon that the infamous highwayman was captured in January 1739. As 'John Palmer' he had left his native Essex, and in various parts of Lincolnshire had eked out a living as butcher, smuggler, horse-dealer and opportunist before crossing the Humber. At first he set himself up in the Brough area, assuming gentler manners and even hobnobbing with country gentlemen. But social lapses were noted, and suspicions were aroused when he wantonly shot a cockerel and began to boast of previous escapades. According to the notice in the bar of the Green Dragon, when Turpin was cornered here by law officers he escaped through a window but was recaptured after a chase. From Beverley he was conducted for trial to York, where his cell in the Castle Museum can still be seen. On the 7th April 1739, at the age of thirty-four, he was publicly hanged on the Knavesmire, now the racecourse.

Site: the Green Dragon, Welton, just below the church and attractive green. The village is on the A63, six miles (9.5km) west of Hull.

Grid Ref: SE 961274 (Market Weighton, Landranger 106)

'A Town of Wells'

This description of Welton goes back to *Domesday Book* (1086), and is still relevant today.

Below the church, the fountain on the village green dates from 1874 and is a listed building. A shallow beck, picturesque always with ducks, runs alongside the churchyard. Beyond, up Dale Road is the stone-backed Cattle Well Spring of our photograph. Before the days of piped water — the 1930s, in many cases — this spring was of great importance in Welton; and, as the plaque indicates, parishioners still have the right to take water. Behind the adjacent cottage is another well. Further up the road is a derelict water-mill, once used for grinding corn. As you enter Welton Dale, there are two delightful springs complete with fish and water fowl. By the old gamekeeper's cottage, with the Wold rising steeply behind, the water bubbling up is known cryptically as Jesus Water.

Site: Dale Road, Welton. The village may be reached from the busy A63, west of Hessle; or via the scenic route of the B1231 from Anlaby and Swanland.

Grid Ref: SE 962275 (Market Weighton, Landranger 106)

Beverley

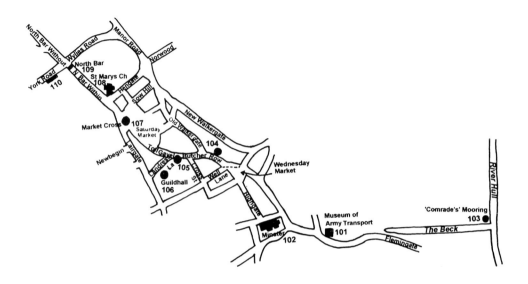

101. Museum of Army Transport
102. Beverley minstrels
103. *Comrade*
104. Crosskill's lamp-post
105. 44 Toll Gavel

106. Guildhall
107. Market cross
108. The Pilgrim Rabbit
109. North Bar
110. Westwood Pastures noticeboards

The Giant Transporter

The entrance to the Museum of Army Transport in Beverley is dominated by this huge Blackburn Beverley transporter aircraft, with a wingspan of 162 feet (49m). It was built at Brough in 1955, and later used at the Royal Aeronautical Establishment at Farnborough for testing brake parachutes and the dropping of men and supplies. It was flown back to Paull airfield, outside Hedon, in 1974 and in due course was dismantled for re-assembly here at Beverley in 1983 as a fitting showpiece for the new museum. Visitors are allowed to climb aboard for a tour of inspection.

The museum teems with fascinating exhibits, including a wagon used by Lord Roberts during the Boer War, the Rolls used by General Montgomery in France and Germany, and modern vehicles that saw service in the Falklands campaign. The exhibitions include a wide range of wartime jobs done by women, uniformed and civilian.

Site: Flemingate, Beverley (B1230).

Grid Ref: TA 043393 (Kingston upon Hull, Landranger 107)

Beverley Minstrels

By Tudor times Beverley had a guild of travelling minstrels. The waits were a group who played in processions and festivals, and who acted also as town watchmen. Three of their ceremonial chains are on view in the Guildhall.

The numerous medieval label-mould carvings on the wall arcade of the Minster's north aisle are claimed to be England's finest collection. The photograph shows players of pipe and drum, but the range and variety of instruments includes horn, bagpipes, shawm, lute and mandolin, tambourine, bell and percussion. Intermixed with the musicians are carvings which show another side to the human condition — lumbago, stomach-ache and toothache! In the choir stalls, the misericords (seats of mercy) are of great interest. No 18 shows an old pig playing the bagpipes while the young ones dance to the music.

In St Mary's Church the Minstrel Pillar (c1520) shows five musical figures in blue and brown, and with long hair and coats. Modern Beverley maintains the tradition with early music and folk festivals.

Site: Beverley Minster is the dominant building on the southern edge of the town.
Grid Ref: TA 042392 (Kingston upon Hull, Landranger 107)

Comrade

Until the 1950s there were still a few keels on the River Humber and its tributaries. The big square sail, plus topsail, were reminiscent of the ancient Viking *coels* — from which 'keels' could have evolved over a thousand years. On windless days they sometimes had to be hauled by horses, or even men, from the canal bank.

This particular vessel, 62 feet (19m) long and with a 15 foot (4.5m) beam, was built as a keel at New Holland, across the Humber. Christened *Wanda*, she spent some years carrying grain to Wakefield and bringing coal back for Hodgson's tannery and the gasworks in Beverley. In 1929 she was bought by Schofields of Beverley, renamed *Comrade* and eventually converted to power.

But gradually she fell from use, and lingered until she was acquired in 1974 by the Humber Keel and Sloop Preservation Society and lovingly re-rigged as a keel. Two years later she was again plying the Humber waters, and is used for short excursions on the rivers and canals of Yorkshire and North Lincolnshire. Her base, however, remains in Beverley.

Site: off Flemingate (B1230) at the east end of Beverley Beck, near the lock gates at the junction with the River Hull.

Grid Ref: TA 056394 (Kingston upon Hull, Landranger 107)

Lamp Posts and Clod Crushers

William Crosskill was one of Beverley's — and Yorkshire's — great Victorian entrepreneurs. His Cart and Wagon Company prospered and he went on to build a huge ironworks off Mill Lane, which by 1853 employed 800 men. Soon afterwards, however, when the firm met cash-flow problems, Crosskill left the business to his sons and retired to Walkergate House (built around 1770), where he died in 1888. As the plaque on this fine residence reminds us, Crosskill was 'father of the East Riding's mechanised farming', and, incidentally, of the clod crusher.

Part of his visible legacy to the town, and from his earlier period, are a number of cast iron lamp-posts, bearing his name at the bottom. One

may be located, amongst several rivals, by the front of the Minster. This one in our photograph stands on Butcher Row, by the Angel Inn. Moreover, they still work, and Crosskill remains a luminary!

Site: Butcher Row is a pedestrianised street off the north side of Wednesday Market, Beverley.

Grid Ref: TA 034395 (Kingston upon Hull, Landranger 107)

44
Toll Gavel

It is rare to find an unfamiliar and puzzling trade sign on a shop. Barbers' poles are well understood, and three brass balls have made a comeback . . . but snakes? Certainly this shop doorway at number forty-four has been an *eye*-catcher since about 1830. On either side, a snake is twisted around these slender portals, its head peering down fairly benignly. But then, a chemist's shop needs to be welcoming: the snakes were the trade signs of Aesclepias, the Greek god of medicine. In recent times the chemist and his potions have moved elsewhere, but the snakes remain.

With regard to the street, *gafol* was Old English for tolls or tribute. In past times, payments were demanded of traders wishing to set up stalls in this street. Nowadays they seem to flourish on the nearby Saturday and Wednesday markets.

Site: Toll Gavel is one of Beverley's central shopping streets.

Grid Ref: TA 033397 (Kingston upon Hull, Landranger 107)

'An Elegant Courtroom'

Sir Alec Clifton-Taylor's phrase, describing Beverley's Guildhall courtroom, is apt. Centre-stage over the dais is the rich coat-of-arms of George III, with the motto of the Order of the Garter, and a lion and a unicorn as supporting figures. An ornate plasterwork ceiling in blue and white by Guiseppe Cortese depicts Justice complete with scales and sword, but curiously *un*blindfolded. Over the public seats at the back is the Beverley crest — a beaver set over a lake, constituting the former name 'Beverlac'. Repairs to the rear wall in 1982 have exposed the fourteenth-century timber-frame of the original house. There has been a guild house on this site since 1320, and the present building was erected in 1762.

Outside the courtroom and at the end of the corridor is a recreated Victorian office. Upstairs in the magistrates room is a pewter dinner service, c1700; and in the mayor's parlour, a board listing all Beverley's mayors since 1573, when the town obtained borough status.

Site: the Guildhall, Register Square, Beverley.

Grid Ref: TA 034396 (Kingston upon Hull, Landranger 107)

Queen Of The Market

Designed by Shelton of Wakefield, Beverley's market cross is octagonal, with eight columns supporting a Baroque dome. It was built between 1711 and 1714 to replace an earlier structure, through which, apparently, a coach and four could be driven. Nowadays, surrounding steps prevent both 'through traffic' and unsightly parking under the dome!

On the southern side, two coats-of-arms are displayed together: those of Queen Anne; and the characteristic beaver and lake ('Beverlac') of the town. Beverley's two MPs of the period also have their shields — on the south- west corner, Sir Charles Hotham (five blue bars, a central red glove and a bird on gold, top left); and the Warton device, an inverted blue chevron on a gold background.

While the cross is architecturally decorative, it provides a focus for the busy Saturday market, and a forum for such public events as processions, a military march-past or as a bandstand. Few towns, even in Yorkshire, can match it!

Site: the Saturday market, Beverley, is the town centre.

Grid Ref: TA 033397 (Kingston upon Hull), Landranger 107)

The Pilgrim Rabbit

The superb west front of St Mary's Church, Beverley, will remind many visitors of King's College Chapel, Cambridge.

Inside, along the north aisle, above the doorway to the sacristy, rests this captivating statuette of a rabbit; because he carries a staff and satchel, he has been dubbed the Pilgrim Rabbit. Although its origins are unknown, it has produced an interesting sequel. Lewis Carroll, creator of *Alice in Wonderland*, was an occasional visitor to the East Riding, and may well have attended services in this church. His grandfather was a customs officer in Hull and an uncle, Henry Lutwidge, was rector at Burton Agnes. Here, surely, in St Mary's is the model and inspiration for the White Rabbit of *Alice*, illustrated so vigorously by Sir John Tenniell.

Above the doorway to the priest's room, note the Beverley Imp.

Site: North Bar Within, Beverley.

Grid Ref: TA 032398 (Kingston upon Hull, Landranger 107)

The North Bar

Medieval Beverley had no town wall, but a ditch with drawbridges at Newbegin, Flemingate, Keldgate, Norwood and the North Bar. This last, thought to be the oldest brick gateway in the country, was rebuilt in 1409 at a cost of £96 0s 11$\frac{1}{2}$d, as the plaque explains. From the main thoroughfare, traffic still passes under the vaulted archway into North Bar Without (an exquisite name!), and on to Malton and Driffield. Between 1934 and 1960 the East Yorkshire Motor Services designed a specially-tapered 'Beverley Bar roof' for their double-decker buses to allow safe negotiation of the North Bar. Heavy gates remain under the bar but are rarely, if ever, used.

For forty-two years the adjoining Bar House was the home of the renowned artist, Frederick Elwell RA. His father James ran a wood-carving business at Nos 4 and 6 North Bar Without. Above No 4's door is a splendidly-executed carved cartoon featuring the Victorian prime minister, Disraeli — 'The political Cheapjack'.

Site: The North Bar separates North Bar Within and North Bar Without, Beverley, at the junctions of the A1035 and A164.

Grid ref: TA 030399 (Kingston upon Hull, Landranger 107)

Where Cows May Safely Graze

Further to a bequest by Neville, Archbishop of York, six centuries ago, these 504 acres (204ha) of the Westwood Pastures have been enjoyed by subsequent generations of Beverlonians. At various times the pastures have provided chalk for streets and buildings, lime, clay, bricks, wood and always pasturage. Once there were five corn-mills, one tower of which, Black Mill, survives.

Twelve pasture masters, locally elected, meet every March to review the grazing arrangements. Comprehensive byelaws deriving authority from the 1836 Pastures Act are inscribed on these boards erected where the open grazing land begins a stone's throw west of the North Bar. In practice, only cows are turned out to graze!

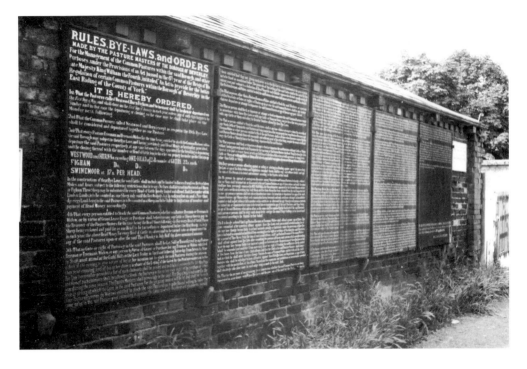

Further up this York Road, Beverley Racecourse, has been in business since 1765. Opposite the west gates is Burton Bushes, still on the Westwood, a preserved area of medieval woodland with oak, birch, ash, maple and holly predominating. Since 1983 these twenty-six acres (10.5ha) have been a Site of Special Scientific Interest.

Site: Beverley, York Road, A1035

Grid Ref: TA 029398 (Kingston upon Hull, Landranger 107)

Further Reading

East Yorkshire Federation of Women's Institutes, *The East Yorkshire Village Book*. Countryside Books, 1991.

J Danby, *Enjoying more of lesser known East Yorkshire*. Highgate Publications, 1990.

C Emett, *Walking the Wolds*. Cicerone Press, 1993.

C Hayes, *Greetings from the Yorkshire Coast*. Printwide Publications, 1992.

Humberside Countryside Packs, published by the technical services department, County Hall, Beverley.

J Markham, *Hedon and Holderness*. Highgate Publications, 1994.

L Markham, *Clarty Strands*. Hutton Press, 1990.

D & T Smith, *North and East Yorkshire Curiosities*. Dovecote Press, 1993.

B Waites, *Exploring the Yorkshire Wolds*. Dalesman Publications, 1984.

G N Wright, *Yorkshire — The East Riding*. Batsford, 1978.

Index